T0049717

FACTOLOGY
ANCIENT EGYPT

Open up a world of information!

ARE YOU READY TO EXPLORE...

Humans haven't changed that drastically throughout the millennia... sure, we have plenty of tech now, and we'd like to think that we're the most sophisticated we've ever been, but at our core, we've remained more or less consistent over time.

This is seen when looking back to the innovative ancient Egyptians, who not only survived but also thrived over the course of 3,000-odd years and had the ability to create tons of amazing art, as well as a pretty progressive society, even by today's standards.

In this book you can discover the ways of this ground-breaking civilisation, including their beliefs about the afterlife and the gods, their fantastic pharaohs, pioneering medicine, astonishing structures and much, much more!

CHAPTER 1

EPIC EGYPT

The land of ancient Egypt was a fascinating place, where people led lives very different to those we lead today. Who were the all-powerful pharaohs that ruled over this complex civilisation? How did ordinary Egyptians eat, treat illnesses or communicate with each other? And why was the river Nile so central to their lives? Let's step back in time more than 4,000 years and find out…

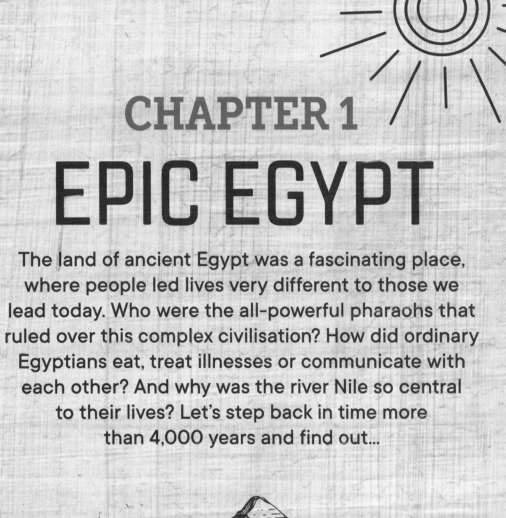

ANCIENT EGYPT THROUGH THE AGES

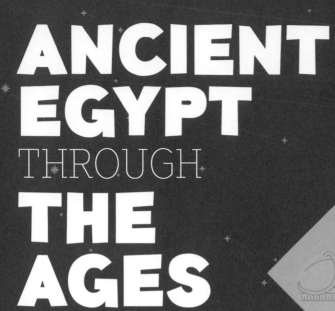

Period called the Old Kingdom

People worship the Sun god Ra

2575 BC
Great pyramids of Giza and Sphinx are built

First pyramid built by Pharaoh Djoser and famous Egyptian architect Imhotep

Hieroglyphic writing invented

1325 BC
King Tutankhamun buried in Valley of Kings

2925 BC
Menes becomes the first pharaoh of Egypt

1279 BC
Pharaoh Ramesses II is greatest ruler of Egypt, reigns for 66 years

332 BC
Alexander the Great conquers Egypt and builds Alexandria

525 BC
Persians take control of Egypt in the Battle of Pelusium

DID YOU KNOW?

It's thought settlers first lived around the Sahara Desert around **9000 BC.**

Back then it had land fit for agriculture but over time became overgrazed, so people started migrating to the lush Nile River Valley, around **6000 BC,** eventually setting up permanent residence.

■ CAIRO

EGYPT

Nile

1975 BC
Start of the Middle Kingdom

Irrigation is used for the first time, carrying water from the Nile to crops

Pharaoh Amenhotep III builds Temple of Luxor

1640 BC
Horse and chariot introduced

Pharaoh Thutmose I is first tomb in Valley of Kings

305 BC
Ptolemy I is pharaoh and Ptolemaic dynasty begins

Hatshepsut is successful female pharaoh, rules for 22 years

1520 BC
Start of the New Kingdom

196 BC
The Rosetta Stone is issued in three different languages in Memphis

30 BC
Last pharaoh, Cleopatra VII Thea Philopator, dies

ALONG THE NILE

This famous waterway brought life to ancient Egypt and connected it to the rest of the world

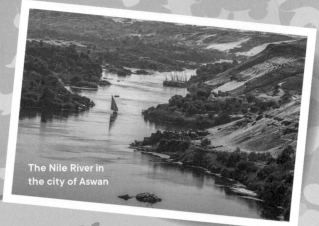

The Nile River in the city of Aswan

BUSY RIVER

Without its fresh water, ancient Egypt simply wouldn't have existed. Even 7,000 years ago, people were farming and trading on the banks of the Nile. This great river flows south to north through Egypt to the Mediterranean Sea and travellers from all over the world passed through. Setting up cities is thirsty work! All of ancient Egypt's major settlements sprang up close to the Nile thanks to its natural resources. The Nile's super soil let farmers grow wheat, flax and papyrus. Anything that couldn't be eaten was turned into clothes and tools. Nothing went to waste!

ALEXANDRIA
PoRT SaiD
SUEZ
CAIRO
SINAI
GIZA
1
Riya
Al MinYa
LuxoR
Dahla
1UT
MaRSa AlaM
AsWaN
Abu SiMBel
Lake NaSSer

ALL ABOARD!

Boats woven from papyrus reeds were lightweight and easy to build. This meant ancient fishermen could get around fast! It wasn't all work though, boats seem to have been used for fun too – there is evidence that Egyptians held boat-jousting tournaments on the river!

RISING TIDES

Ancient Egyptians based their seasons around the Nile's changing tides. The year began in summer when its banks would flood. Modern Egyptians still celebrate the Nile's flooding every August!

FAST FACTS

1 The Nile is 6,650km long – that's almost seven times the length of the UK!

x7

2 It flows through 11 countries and has 3 main tributaries that flow into it.

3 Every second the Nile spits out 3.1 million litres of water – that's more water than in an Olympic-sized swimming pool!

4 It has a depth of between 8m and 11m, and at its widest measures nearly 3km across.

5 To this day over 95% of Egypt lives just kilometres from the Nile!

95%

6 It's not just humans that use the Nile to get around, it's home to hundreds of species – from tiny fish to massive mammals like hippos and rhinos.

7 North of Cairo the Nile splits into two streams – the west's Rosetta Branch and the east's Damietta.

8 The word 'Nile' means **GREAT RIVER** in Greek.

GIFTS FROM THE GODS

Ancient Egyptians believed the gods had blessed them with the gift of the Nile. Some of the temples they built in their honour are still standing today. Temples were built on the river's west banks to welcome the Sun god Ra as he set.

Land of the
Pharaohs

Ancient Egypt had to have had some pretty powerful rulers for the civilisation to continue strong for 3,000-odd years. Here are 10 of the most exciting...

OLD KINGDOM
Thriving civilisation and stable government, lots of pyramids built in this time.

2575–2150 BC

MENES

Other names: Narmer
Dynasty: 1st
Around in: 2925 BC
Ruled for: 62 years
Notable achievement: Unified Upper and Lower Egypt, kicking off millennia of dynasties and rule. Founded Memphis – the capital of ancient Egypt during the Old Kingdom.
Death: Killed by a hippo.

DJOSER

Other names: Zoser
Dynasty: 3rd
Around in: 2630 BC
Ruled for: 18 years
Notable achievement: Commissioned loads of cool architecture built by his whizz minister Imhotep, such as the Step Pyramid at Saqqara – the first large stone building and prototype of later pyramids.
Death: Unknown cause, buried in the Step Pyramid.

KHAFRE

Other names: Khafra, Chephren (Greek)
Dynasty: 4th
Around in: 2575 BC
Ruled for: 26 years
Notable achievement: Following in father Khufu's footsteps, he had the second of three Giza pyramids built. The Great Sphinx's face is thought to be modelled after him.
Death: Unknown cause, buried in his own pyramid.

KHUFU

Other names: Khnum-Khufwy, Cheops (Greek)
Dynasty: 4th
Around in: 2589 BC
Ruled for: Anywhere from 23–34, to 63 years
Notable achievement: Commissioned the Great Pyramid at Giza – largest one ever built and the first at that location.
Death: Unknown cause, buried in the Great Pyramid.

NEW KINGDOM

1520–1075 BC

Golden age of ancient Egypt, a period of great wealth, prosperity and power.

HATSHEPSUT

Other names: Hatchepsut
Dynasty: 18th
Around in: 1478 BC
Ruled for: 21 years
Notable achievement: Most successful female pharaoh and all-round awesome ruler under whose rule, Egypt thrived.
Death: Accidentally gave herself bone cancer while attempting to treat a skin condition with a moisturising lotion that contained a chemical found in tar.

MIDDLE KINGDOM

1975–1640 BC

A short stable era sandwiched by two periods of political upheaval. A time when Osiris was the most important god.

SENUSRET I

Other names: Kheperkare, Sesostris, Senwosret
Dynasty: 12th
Around in: 1918 BC
Ruled for: 33 years
Notable achievement: One of the most powerful kings of this dynasty, he did loads of good political moves that benefited Egyptians and also commissioned a ton of interesting buildings.
Death: Unknown cause.

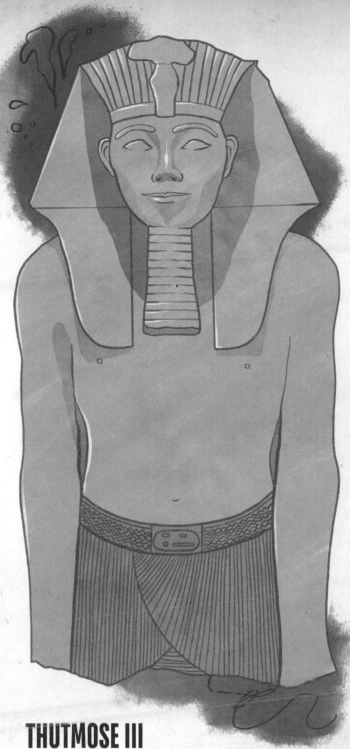

AMENHOTEP III

Other names: Amenhotep the Magnificent
Dynasty: 18th
Around in: 1388 BC
Ruled for: 39 years
Notable achievement: King Tut's grandad, has the most surviving statues of any pharaoh – over 250 have been found so far. He also improved Egypt's economy and had loads of monuments and statues built, such as Luxor Temple.
Death: Unknown cause, buried in the Valley of the Kings.

THUTMOSE III

Other names: Tuthmosis, Thothmes
Dynasty: 18th
Around in: 1450 BC
Ruled for: 54 years
Notable achievement: A skilled warrior who created the largest empire Egypt had ever seen.
Death: Natural causes.

AKHENATEN

Other names: Amenhotep IV, Amenophis (Greek), the Heretic King
Dynasty: 18th
Around in: 1350 BC
Ruled for: 17 years
Notable achievement: Father of King Tut, he went against tradition and established a new cult dedicated to a single god – Aton (he changed his name from Amenhotep IV to Akhenaten, which means 'beneficial to Aton').
Death: Unknown cause, missing body.

RAMESSES II

Other names: Ramses the Great
Dynasty: 19th
Around in: 1270 BC
Ruled for: 66 years
Notable achievement: Second longest reign in Egyptian history, had a flourishing military career and died at ripe old age of 90 – which is a huge achievement now, let alone in those days!
Death: Suffocation.

A DAY IN THE LIFE

Want to live as an ancient Egyptian pharaoh for the day? Here's your schedule...

6:00 Wake up at dawn, along with the sun god Ra.

6:15 Get your servants to give you a clean, shave your head, put kohl around your eyes and dab some perfumed oil on you. They'll also dress you in a classic outfit of a white linen, knee-length robe, fastened with a buckle at the waist, and put on your jewellery, such as a gold falcon chest piece. Don't forget your headdress! Now you're ready for the day.

7:30 Breakfast of bread, fruit and beer in the courtyard, accompanied by your main wife.

8:00 Receive visitors to the audience chamber, to kickstart the day's official business. Accept gifts from foreign ambassadors, give approval for building or irrigation projects, discuss military matters, make laws, order death penalties for wrongdoers.

10:30 Go to perform rituals at a nearby temple to keep evil spirits away from Egypt.

12:00 Lunchtime! Your royal spread includes meat, wine, fruit and veg, as well as an indulgent bread flavoured with honey, nuts and dates.

13:30 After lunch, stroll in the palace garden, among fig trees, date palms, terraces and pools.

14:00 Play a board game with your children.

14:30 Have a check-up with the royal doctor, who might cure your ailments with a spell or two.

15:00 Go hunting or fishing – the more exotic the animal caught, the better.

18:00 For dinner, it's a royal banquet, while being entertained by dancers and musicians playing harps, lutes, drums, tambourines and clappers. Guests include important noble people and members of the royal family. Wine is flowing and food might include something caught on the day's hunt – such as ox. Dessert is fruit, including dates, figs, plums and melons.

23:00 Bedtime! Leave the banquet and make your way to your bedroom at the rear of the palace. Sleep safe with the knowledge that you're being protected from evil spirits by magic, as well as your bodyguards.

DID YOU KNOW?
A dynasty refers to a period of time where a civilisation is ruled by a succession of rulers from a common group, usually the same family line. It's widely accepted that ancient Egypt had around 30.

WONDER *WOMAN*

Female pharaohs were few and far between, but considered the greatest of them all – who could give many male rulers a run for their money – was the mighty Hatshepsut who reigned for more than two decades

Family fortunes

Hatshepsut married her half-brother Thutmose II, taking over as ruler after his death. By tradition, the position would go to Thutmose II's son, Thutmose III (yes, they weren't too imaginative with names), but as he was just an infant at the time, Hatshepsut stepped up to the job.

MARRIED HALF-BROTHER

Super trader

One of Hatshepsut's greatest achievements was setting sail to a distant land called Punt for the first time in 500 years and bringing back all sorts of goodies for ancient Egyptians, such as gold, ivory, live myrrh trees and exotic animals, including apes, panthers and giraffes.

What do you call an Egyptian back doctor? A Cairo-practor!

DID YOU KNOW?
Hatshepsut preferred to be portrayed as a man, with a broader body, bulging muscles and a fake beard.

COLOSSAL STRUCTURES

One of the ancient world's most impressive architectural structures, Hatshepsut's memorial temple Djeser-Djeseru – meaning 'holy of holies' – was decked out with murals depicting scenes from her reign as well as shrines to various gods such as Anubis, Hathor, Amun and Ra.

DID YOU KNOW?

A powerful and intelligent leader, the time during Hatshepsut's reign was a prosperous one for ancient Egypt.

Removed from history

After Hatshepsut died, the throne went to Thutmose III in 15th century BC, who tried to destroy all evidence of her existence. He removed her image from monuments and statues, and erased her from the official list of Egyptian rulers – luckily he didn't do a very good job so archaeologists were able to rediscover her as an important ruler.

File name:

TOP SECRET

File No.

FIVE FORMIDABLE
FEMALE PHARAOHS

Merneith
Egypt's first recorded female leader ruled for almost a decade around 2950 BC, stepping up to the job on behalf of her young son after her husband King Djet died.

Sobekneferu
The last ruler of the 12th dynasty (around 1760 BC) was in charge for almost four years but died without an heir, bringing the Golden Age of the Middle Kingdom to a close.

Nefertiti
Whether the wife of the 'Heretic King' Akhenaten actually ruled in her own right after his death in 1350 BC is much debated, but what's certain is that she has been depicted as equal to a king in many archaeological sites.

Twosret
The final pharaoh of the 19th Dynasty, Twosret's tomb was found in the Valley of the Kings and suggests that she held significant power.

Cleopatra VII
Arguably the most famous female pharaoh, Cleopatra's death in 30 BC marked the end of the ancient Egyptian civilisation.

RECORD-SMASHING Ramesses II

Considered the greatest pharaoh of Egypt, Ramesses II, also known as Ramesses the Great, was a formidable warrior and prolific builder – not to mention a massive show-off!

LONG-SERVING LEADER

The third king of the 19th Dynasty, Ramesses II had the second-longest reign in Egyptian history – he ruled for a whopping 66 years. He became Prince of Egypt at the age of 15 and was crowned pharaoh at 25 when his dad Seti I died.

SAME NAMES

Ramesses II was the son of Pharaoh Seti I and Queen Tuya. He was named after Seti's dad Ramesses I, whose dad (so Ramesses II's great-grandad) was also called Seti... which would have made family get-togethers pretty chaotic!

RAMESSES II ON AN EGYPTIAN BANKNOTE

FATHERED NEARLY 200 CHILDREN

RULED FOR 66 YEARS

BRUTAL BATTLES

Since the age of 22, Ramesses was leading his own battles against various enemies of Egypt, such as the Hittites, Syrians, Libyans and Nubians. One of these was the Battle of Kadesh.

DID YOU KNOW?

Historians think there could have been

UP TO **3,500 CHARIOTS** ON BOTH SIDES

and as many as

30,000 WARRIORS IN THE BATTLE OF KADESH

WHAT ABOUT
SLAVES?

When the rulers of ancient Egypt didn't want to get their hands dirty, they made their people do the hard work for them!

BAD BOSSES

Slaves didn't have it easy! Pharaohs and rulers with enough power were able to make the people of ancient Egypt do whatever they wanted.

NASTY MASTERS

How slaves were treated depended on the nature of their owners. Most masters treated slaves like property but some were kinder. The rights of slaves evolved over time. They eventually could leave if their masters were cruel.

SLAVES IN NUMBERS

How many ancient Egyptians were slaves? **AROUND 10%**

How long did slaves work? **16 HOURS PER DAY**

When did the first slaves exist? **AROUND 6800 BC**

An engraving showing roped slaves on the stone wall leading into the Great Temple of Ramesses II at Abu Simbel built between 1274 and 1244 BC

DID YOU KNOW?
Even children could be slaves! Life wasn't very fair for people without money.

HARD WORK
Slaves weren't just made to build huge buildings like temples. Some were kept indoors while some were sent to fight in faraway wars. There's not actually much proof that slaves built the pyramids. The ancient Greeks suggested they did!

ROYAL RESPECT
Slaves of royal and powerful families were more respected than most Egyptians. They'd learn skills like algebra and housekeeping.

MEDICINE MAN

Ancient Egypt is where the concept of health probably started – but their ideas about illness were very different to today...

Imagine this: you go to the doctor with chickenpox – and they give you a magic spell to make you better. Early Egyptian medicine was based on religious spells, so a trip to hospital could seem like being at a magic show! But instead you'd meet a doctor who was a dab-hand at spells and rituals, and they'd certainly be waving a wand around!

Don't worry, this won't hurt a bit...

Luck of the draw
Ancient Egyptians believed disease was not affected by germs or your genes, but by other people's spiteful intentions, for example, or your bad behaviour – or even an angry ghost!

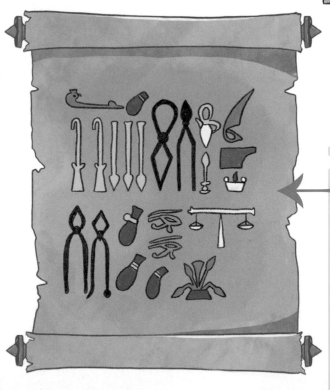

TOOLS of THE TRADE

They had an astounding array of medical and surgical tools – including:

- saws
- forceps
- scales
- shears
- hooks
- spins
- drills
- a measuring rod called a graduated cubit.

We know doctors also did surgery with knives as mention of 'knife treatments' are to be found in the Ebers and Edwin Smith Papyri (page 24).

HOLY, HOLY, HOLY

Your doctor would likely be a priest – because in Egypt, they were the first to practise medicine. Some used herbal remedies and non-surgical treatments, but most 'cures' were still done with magic in the first instance. This all began to change, though, with the rise of one genius...

IMHOTEP – Egyptian superstar!

Born to a humble family in the 27th century BC, Imhotep was a man of many talents. He designed the first and oldest pyramid, the Step Pyramid at Saqqara. But it was his skills as a healer and his ideas about medicine that made him famous. No wonder King Djoser made him chancellor, bestowing incredible powers on him.

Green genius

Imhotep was first to extract medicines from plants. He diagnosed and treated more than 200 medical conditions, and performed surgery and dentistry. He was such a shiny star, that after his death, he was elevated to god-like status and was worshipped at his temple in Memphis.

DIAGNOSED & TREATED 200 MEDICAL CONDITIONS

SURGEON

DENTIST

Doctor, Doctor...

After Imhotep, medicine in ancient Egypt raced ahead. Doctor priests trained at The House of Life, the first school dedicated to the study of medicine. They focused on one disease or body part – if you had an eye problem you saw an eye doctor – like today. They realised disease could be treated with drugs, as well as massage, aromas and keeping hygienic!

TEXT MESSAGES

We also know Egyptians were ahead of the west from medical papyri – ancient texts written by priest physicians. They reveal ideas on disease and diagnosis, herbal remedies and surgery, and treatments used alongside spells and magic.

The most important medical papyri are:

1 EDWIN SMITH: dated circa 1600 BC, and believed to have been written by Imhotep. The oldest surgical text shows how medical practices were changing – surgery was being used instead of 'religious healing' and they knew about trauma (shock to the body or mind). They had an impressive knowledge of anatomy, gained from removing human organs for mummification.

2 EBERS: the largest Egyptian medical document in history, discovered 150 years ago in a junk shop. It contains 700 magical spells and remedies for all kinds of health issues, including mental illnesses – another Egyptian breakthrough.

3 BERLIN: shows they were the first to diagnose symptoms of pregnancy, and be able to tell if a woman was having a boy or a girl.

Tinkling the ivories

The first named dentist was Hesy-Ra, meaning 'Great one of the ivory cutters', who was a high official at the time of Pharaoh Djoser. You can imagine his skills – an artist and 'ivory cutter' would come in handy if the king lost his teeth and needed a new pair of pearlies made... The Egyptians weren't strangers to oral hygiene either, the food they ate was gritty and over time they learned how to protect their teeth with simple frayed stick toothbrushes.

THE GODS HAVE IT

Even after Imhotep, medicine and magic overlapped for some time. The gods still figured in healing, and prayers were sent to deities to repel illness.

There were three main gods of medicine:

THOTH　　**SEKHMET**　　**ISIS**

ANCIENT REMEDIES

The Egyptians knew some diseases, such as malaria or cancer, were still beyond their knowledge and skills. But that didn't stop them treating conditions with native remedies, for example:

ASTHMA	honey and milk, sesame, frankincense
HEADACHES	poppy seeds, aloe
BURNS AND SKIN DISEASES	aloe
PAIN RELIEF	thyme
DIGESTIVE AIDS	juniper, mint, garlic, sandalwood
BREATH FRESHENER	caraway, mint
CHEST PAINS	mustard seeds, aloe, juniper
DRESSING A WOUND	honey (natural antibiotic)
LAXATIVES	onions, parsley, balsam apple, dill
VOMITING	mint to stop it, mustard seeds to induce it.

Oh, and not forgetting a novel remedy prescribed in the Ebers Papyrus – **'CURE FOR DEATH'**: take 'a froth of beer and half an onion'!

Channel hopping

Doctors once believed bad 'spirits' blocked channels in the body, causing problems. This theory came from watching farmers dig irrigation channels for their crops. Channels would be 'cleared' with prayer and even laxatives! Still, this led to the idea that the channels carried fluid – as veins, arteries or intestines do. It was a major turning point moving from spiritual cures to practical ones.

POPPY SEEDS

ALOE

ONION

HONEY

THYME

CARAWAY

Ancient diets

What's a mummy's favourite food? Wraps! But the honest truth is Egyptians had very specific and (some say) advanced ideas about how diet affects health. They realised to avoid infection in their hot climate and before fridges were invented it would be safer to avoid eating 'unclean' foods, including raw fish. So definitely don't pass the sushi!

State of the ART

The ancient Egyptians weren't too busy building and surviving to be creative! Archaeologists have found all sorts of art spanning 2,700 years including paper drawings, jewellery and pottery...

❋The ancient Egyptians didn't have a word for 'art' like we do today. Rather than the art we make for fun, much of their work related to the gods and pharaohs. It's more like merchandise!

SHINE ON

The Egyptians used a blue faience glaze to amplify something's beauty permanently. Things glossed in this way were considered to contain the shimmer of the sun and power of rebirth. The glaze was made from quartz, alkaline salts, lime and other minerals and was an inexpensive way to imitate the rare turquoise – a semi-precious stone. It was often used on ceramic creations such as small figures of gods and animals, amulets and jewellery.

MAKING PAPER

Ancient Egyptians made very strong paper using the papyrus plant. Today we use machinery to make wood pulp – back then, they blended tiny fibres with water from the Nile. The pharaohs knew they had something special! The best papyrus mixtures were closely guarded and their creators were hired by the state to make perfect parchment. The ancient Egyptians were so good at making paper that they sold their parchment recipes to other nations!

Reed rediscovery

While the ancient Egyptians made papyrus paper very well, nobody wrote it down! The art form was lost until 1965 when historian Dr Hassan Ragab started to grow his own.

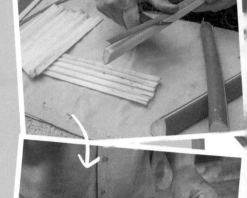

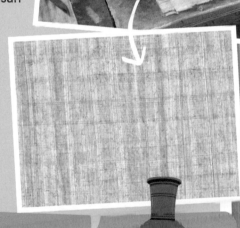

Protective pendants

Jewellery is still used to show off today but in ancient Egypt craftsmen wore pendants and badges that told others who they were. Special messages even asked the gods for protection.

DID YOU KNOW?

It's not just paper ancient Egyptians could make with papyrus! They also wove its fibres to make sails, sandals and mats.

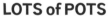

Did you know?

Master crafters were not allowed to sign their work like today – but bringing the best items to the market was a brilliant boast!

LOTS of POTS

Why do you think pottery was so important? In the dry and dusty desert, protecting your things was crucial! Earthenware pottery could be forged easily using readily available, natural materials.

Shop 'til ya DROP

Ancient Egyptians from all walks of life would find bargains and trade in the markets – from food and drink, to arts, crafts and other important goods. What have you got to trade?

Meet in the market

In ancient Egypt, every city had a bustling marketplace where people would go shopping for food and supplies. Can you imagine how noisy the vibrant markets would have been?

A deben

3 OUNCES
THE WEIGHT OF A DEBEN SCALE

Swap shop

The ancient Egyptians didn't use money like we do today. Farmers would bring animals, crops, fruit and vegetables to trade while craftspeople would make furniture, ornaments and toys.

DID YOU KNOW?

Ancient Egyptians used a set of scales called a deben to make sure trades were fair.

WHEN WAS THE EARLIEST MONEY INTRODUCED?

Tomb paintings show ancient Egypt royalty tucking into honey-roasted deer, delicately prepared duck and foreign fruits that would have been hard to find... Meals fit for a king and queen!

Food for fuel

Workers and their families ate two meals a day and were able to cook like we do. Ingredients may have been more scarce but people still ate bread, meat and vegetables to stay active.

ACTIVITIES

Eat like an Egyptian

Ask a parent or guardian if you can try raw garlic, figs or dates. Egyptians loved them!

Seller story

Write a short story about a day in the life of an ancient shopkeeper.

Coin count

How many hidden coins can you find on this spread?

600 BC

In other words

Want to learn a language? Writing with pictures was an easy way for any ancient Egyptian to understand what was going on...

1   **10**   **100**   **1,000**   **10,000**   **100,000**   **1,000,000**

Count to ten

The ancient Egyptians had a decimal system – just like us! Rounding up makes it easier to keep track of large numbers of crops, workers or even riches. There's a symbol for 1, 10, 100, 1,000, 10,000, 100,000 and even 1 million. If you wanted multiples, say, 20, you'd just use two of the symbol for 10!

Historic hieroglyphs

We wouldn't have the English alphabet today without ancient Egyptians paving the way! Imagine our language without its rules on which way to read across a page. As time moved on, so did hieroglyphs.

Old school

This system's been around for 5,000 years and yet we still remember it. Most people then couldn't read or write like today, so it was important that hieroglyphs were easy to understand for everyone.

VERY IMPORTANT

QUITE IMPORTANT

NOT VERY IMPORTANT

Size matters

Scale meant everything to the ancient Egyptians! The bigger someone was in a picture or a statue, the more important they were. Archaeologists have learned a lot by looking at the smallest subjects.

Sketch relic

Find an ancient relic like a plaque or a monument. Grab some paper and a crayon and rub over it to make your own copy.

4,000 LIVING WRITTEN LANGUAGES EXIST IN THE WORLD TODAY

DID YOU KNOW?

There was a shorthand version used for bartering called hieratic that was written on papyrus.

700 CHARACTERS HAVE BEEN DISCOVERED IN HIEROGLYPHICS

DID YOU KNOW?

Hieroglyphs were literally called 'the words of the gods'.

BATTLE READY

A generally peaceful civilisation, the ancient Egyptians didn't have much warfare experience and mostly only fought to defend themselves. Turn over to discover three of the biggest battles they ever fought...

CHOOSE YOUR FIGHTER

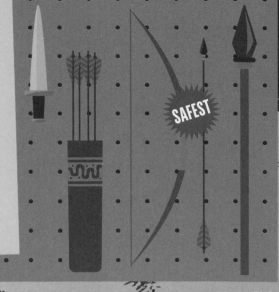

Soldiers trained with weapons such as swords, knives, spears, bows and arrows, and used their best one in battle. Many trained harder to be an archer as they had the safest position away from the frontlines.

SAFEST

FACT One of the first documented battles in history.

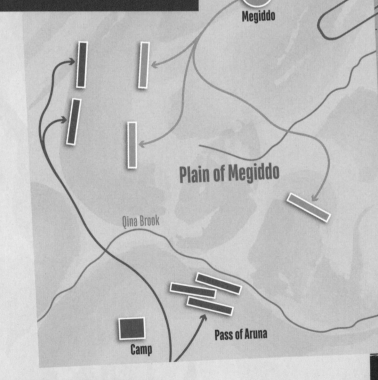

Megiddo

Plain of Megiddo

Qina Brook

Pass of Aruna

Camp

THE BATTLE OF
MEGIDDO

When: 1479 BC

Who: THUTMOSE III vs REBEL EGYPTIAN KINGS *(Canaanites of Megiddo)*

Why: Rebels thought Thutmose was a weak leader so tried to overthrow him.

What happened: Thutmose III resisted the attacking forces and held the rebel cities under a seven-month siege.

Winner: Thutmose III

Aftermath: Expanded Egyptian territory.

IN THE ARMY? EXPECT RESPECT...
Soldiers could be away for months at a time in battle and were well-regarded by ancient Egyptians. They were given land and treasure by the pharaoh in return for their difficult training and time.

THE BATTLE OF
PELUSIUM

When: 525 BC

Who: PSAMTIK III vs PERSIANS

Why: Persians wanted control of Egypt.

What happened: Persian king Cambyses II knew how much the Egyptians loved cats so used them in battle to throw the soldiers off their game. We're not quite sure whether the Persians used real cats while they were fighting or just painted the animals on their shields but we know that the Egyptians, not wanting to offend their goddess Bastet, fled to Memphis where they surrendered.

Winner: Persians

Aftermath: Persians took control of Egypt.

FACT One of the earliest forms of psychological warfare.

THE BATTLE OF
KADESH

When: 1274 BC

Who: RAMESSES II vs THE HITTITES

Why: For control of Syrian city Kadesh, one of great strategic importance. Ramesses wanted to recapture it from the Hittites.

What happened: Ramesses II was lured into a trap by two Hittite spies and got cut off from his troops but managed to rally them and corner the Hittites.

Winner: Draw – Ramesses II won the battle but didn't conquer Kadesh.

Aftermath: World's first peace treaty signed and the two nations had a mutually beneficial trading relationship.

FACT One of the world's largest chariot battles.

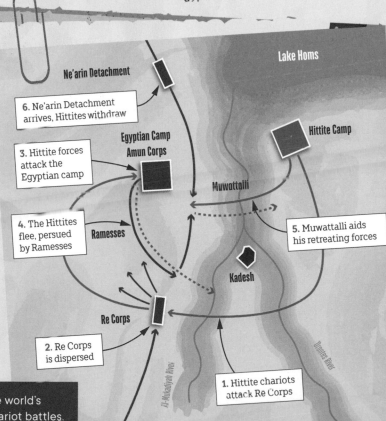

1. Hittite chariots attack Re Corps

2. Re Corps is dispersed

3. Hittite forces attack the Egyptian camp

4. The Hittites flee, persued by Ramesses

5. Muwattalli aids his retreating forces

6. Ne'arin Detachment arrives, Hittites withdraw

Ne'arin Detachment

Lake Homs

Egyptian Camp
Amun Corps

Hittite Camp

Muwattalli

Ramesses

Kadesh

Re Corps

Family fortunes

To make life simple (or more confusing) all boys in the Ptolemaic dynasty were named Ptolemy (pronounced tol-uh-mee) and girls were called Cleopatra, Berenice or Arsinoe — Cleopatra was actually the seventh one in her family!

'Hi, we're Ptolemy'

69 BC
Cleopatra VII is born in Alexandria, Egypt

61 BC
Cleo's little brother Ptolemy XIII is born

54 BC
Caesar invades Britain

52 BC
Cleo is co-ruler of Egypt with her dad

51 BC
Cleo's dad dies, she's made queen with 10-year-old brother Ptolemy XIII

QUEEN of the NILE

30 BC
Antony and Cleo commit suicide

31 BC
The Battle of Actium

Fight for the fate of Rome

The two armies met in a tremendous sea fight called the Battle of Actium. It raged all morning until Cleopatra, worried they were losing, turned and fled the scene, taking her ships with her. Antony managed to escape, but most of his fleet was burnt or sunk and Octavian was declared master of the Roman world.

While Cleopatra is famously associated with ancient Egypt, she wasn't actually Egyptian – she was Greek! But she spoke the language fluently and was one of the first in the Ptolemaic dynasty to do so...

Oh brother!

When Cleo was 18, her dad died. He left Cleo and her 10-year-old brother Ptolemy XIII in charge, expecting them to rule Egypt together. But instead, they fought for the title of ruler.

Bad blood

Cleo took Little Caesar to visit his dad, but the Romans weren't happy about it! Caesar already had a wife, and they were worried he might try to make Alexandria the new Roman capital.

50 BC
Cleo says she's main ruler and stamps her face on all new coins

49 BC
Ptolemy gets angry and kicks her out of Egypt

48 BC
Cleo sneaks into Caesar's room rolled in a rug

47 BC
Caesar says Cleo is Queen again. She gives birth to Little Caesar

44 BC
Romans kill Caesar. Cleo rules with Little Caesar

Love games

Cleo knew she needed legendary Roman general Julius Caesar on her side. So when she heard that Caesar was in Alexandria, she decided to try and win him over. To avoid her brother's guards, Cleo snuck into Caesar's room rolled in a rug!

On the run

On 15 March, a group of 60 Roman senators stabbed Caesar 23 times. Cleo was forced to flee back to Egypt. With Caesar dead, two new men took over – Roman general Mark Antony and Caesar's adopted son and heir, Octavian.

32 BC
Rome gets angry, Octavian declares war on Cleo

34 BC
Antony gives land to his and Cleo's kids at Donations of Alexandria

37 BC
Cleo marries Antony

40 BC
Cleo gives birth to twins, Sun and Moon

41 BC
Cleo and Antony meet. Her sister Arsinoe dies

Warmonger

Caesar's other son and heir, Octavian, ruled the western part of Rome's lands. He was so angry when he heard that Antony and Cleo had said Little Caesar was the heir to Rome, he declared war on Cleopatra.

Spoilt rotten!

Antony and Cleopatra were determined their kids would rule the world one day, and invited the whole city of Alexandria to a spectacular celebration, where they divided up Rome's lands between them and told everyone Cleo's oldest son, Little Caesar, was the heir to Rome.

All's fair in love and war

Caesar's death meant Cleo needed a new Roman ally, general Mark Antony was perfect. Egypt was fabulously wealthy but needed protecting from invasion. Rome had a huge army, but needed money to fight wars. So Cleo gave Antony money, and Antony protected Egypt.

CLEOPATRA'S
BEAUTY
Secrets

Instantly recognisable, Cleo's look is iconic. But do we know what she actually looked like?

Cleo's beauty is legendary. Roman historian Cassius Dio said she was 'a woman of surpassing beauty' who was 'brilliant to look upon'. But she's actually the faceless queen – no one really knows what she looked like. Her face does appear on ancient coins, where she looks hook-nosed and manly, but this could have been done on purpose to intimidate her enemies. Whether she was gorgeous or not, we do know the Egyptians were one of the first civilisations to use perfumes, oils and other beauty treatments.

For the Egyptians, make-up was useful as well as beautiful. Kohl (a dark powder used as eyeliner) was said to have anti-bacterial properties and to keep eyes cool in the sun,

EYEBROWS were painted black using burnt almonds

3
 CASTOR
 SESAME
 **MORINGA**

OILS used on the face to combat wrinkles and preserve youth

The milk from
700
donkeys

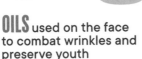
for one milk bath

10% GREASE

probably
GOOSE FAT,
was found in cosmetic powders recovered from the tombs of pharaohs

16
ingredients in kyphi, considered the first perfume ever created, produced from berries, honey, flowers and wine. Kyphi was not just for smelling good though, it's thought it was used in temples to purify the air and used as a medicine for various ailments.

Death of a civilisation

Cleo was the last pharaoh of Egypt, and her death brought to an end one of the world's oldest civilisations. Cleopatra was only 39 when she died, and she had been queen of Egypt for 21 years

What happened?

Her death is shrouded in mystery. She and Antony fled to Egypt after the Battle of Actium. When Octavian's army reached Alexandria, Antony bravely rode to the battlefield to face him, but hearing false news that Cleo had been killed, he fell on his sword. Overcome with grief, Cleo is said to have committed suicide How she did this still isn't clear, though. Stories say an asp – probably an Egyptian cobra – bit her on the arm. Alternatively Greek historian Plutarch says she also hid deadly poison in her hair combs.

I heard people are trying to ban Roman numerals – not on my watch!

DID YOU KNOW?

Cleopatra lived closer to the creation of the iPhone than she did to the building of the Great Pyramid.

The Great Pyramid was built around 2560 BC, while Cleopatra lived around 69-30 BC.

The iPhone was launched in 2007, which is about 500 years closer!

WHAT HAPPENED NEXT?

Octavian took over after Antony and Cleo died, and the Roman Empire was born!

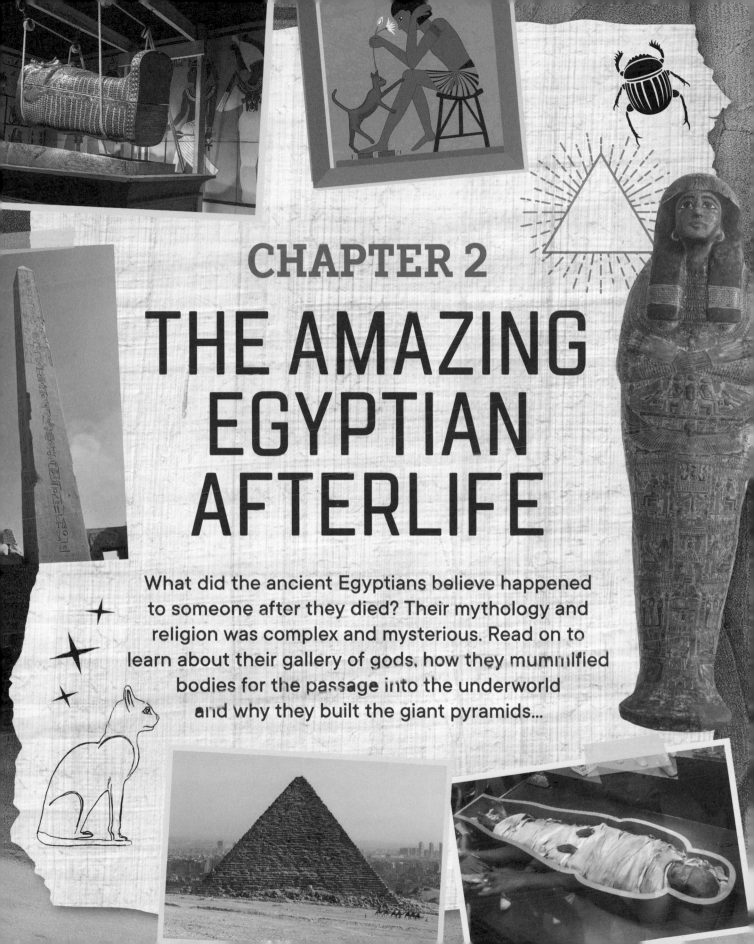

CHAPTER 2

THE AMAZING EGYPTIAN AFTERLIFE

What did the ancient Egyptians believe happened to someone after they died? Their mythology and religion was complex and mysterious. Read on to learn about their gallery of gods, how they mummified bodies for the passage into the underworld and why they built the giant pyramids...

Osiris

God of fertility and the underworld

APPEARANCE

White headdress with feathers

REPRESENTED BY

Crook and flail

DID YOU KNOW?

Ancient Egyptians believed that Osiris gave them the gift of barley, one of their most important crops.

Set

God of war, chaos and storms

APPEARANCE

Head of an unidentifiable animal

REPRESENTED BY

Was-sceptre (see page 49), Set animal

DID YOU KNOW?

The Set animal is thought to be a mixture of an aardvark, a donkey, a jackal or a fennec fox.

Oh my
GODS!

The ancient Egyptians had countless gods and goddesses, who were used in all manner of ways – to explain natural events and called upon for help through rituals. Here are some of the most popular...

Horus

God of the sky and ruler of the world of the living

APPEARANCE

Head of a hawk

REPRESENTED BY

Eye of Horus

DID YOU KNOW?

Horus fought with his uncle Set for the throne of Egypt, where he lost one of his eyes. The eye was restored and became a symbol of protection.

Nut

Goddess of the sky

APPEARANCE

Water pot
on her head

REPRESENTED BY

Stars

DID YOU KNOW?

It was believed that at the end of the day,
Nut swallowed the sun god, Ra, and gave
birth to him again the next morning.

Hapy

God of the annual flooding of the Nile

APPEARANCE

Pot belly

REPRESENTED BY

Lotus plant

DID YOU KNOW?

While Hapy is one of the most popular
and powerful gods of ancient Egypt, no
temple has yet been discovered which
was specifically dedicated to him.

Thoth

God of writing, knowledge and the Moon

APPEARANCE

Head of
an ibis

REPRESENTED BY

Ibis, baboon

DID YOU KNOW?

Thoth is credited with inventing the
365-day calendar, which we use today!

Geb

God of the earth

APPEARANCE

Goose on
his head

REPRESENTED BY

Barley, a goose

DID YOU KNOW?

It was believed that earthquakes were
Geb's laughter.

Sobek

God of the river Nile

APPEARANCE

Head of a crocodile and headdress of feathers

REPRESENTED BY

Crocodile

DID YOU KNOW?

Crocodiles were kept in temples because they were thought to be icons of Sobek on Earth. It was believed that if they accepted your offer of food, you would receive Sobek's blessings.

Hathor

Goddess of love and joy

APPEARANCE

Headdress of horns and a sun disc

REPRESENTED BY

Cow

DID YOU KNOW?

Hathor was strongly linked to turquoise gems, gold and copper, and so was called Mistress of Turquoise.

Amun

God of air

APPEARANCE

Ostrich-plumed hat

REPRESENTED BY

Ram

DID YOU KNOW?

Known as the king of the gods, when Amun was combined with the sun god Ra – to form Amun-Ra – he was even more powerful.

Tefnut

Goddess of the rain

APPEARANCE

Head of a lioness

REPRESENTED BY

Lioness

DID YOU KNOW?

According to mythology, Tefnut was created from the spit of the cosmic creator Atum, along with her twin brother Shu.

Ptah

God of craftsmen and architects

APPEARANCE
Wrapped in a tight white cloak carrying a staff

REPRESENTED BY
Bull

DID YOU KNOW?
The word 'Egypt' comes from the Greek Αγο (Aigyptos), which is believed to derive from the Middle Egyptian wt-ka-ptah, meaning 'House of the Soul of Ptah'.

Nephthys

Goddess of mourning, the night/ darkness, temples

APPEARANCE
Headdress with her name in hieroglyphs

REPRESENTED BY
Sacred temple enclosure

DID YOU KNOW?
Nephthys is often shown on coffins or in funerary scenes.

Khepri

God of creation, movement of the Sun and rebirth

APPEARANCE
Head of a scarab (dung) beetle

REPRESENTED BY
Scarab beetle

DID YOU KNOW?
Just like how scarab beetles push around small balls of dung, it was believed that Khepri was the god who pushed the Sun in its orbit.

Atum

God of creation

APPEARANCE
Double crown

REPRESENTED BY
Serpent

DID YOU KNOW?
Atum was thought to be the first being to emerge from the darkness, energy and matter of chaos.

Feline FIERCE

Daughter of Ra, goddess of the home, women, cats, war, music, the arts and protector from evil spirits and disease, Bastet was a powerful deity who was worshipped all over the country

Why cats?

Lions, panthers and jungle cats could be found in the wild in Egypt, but people also kept smaller ones as pets. This is mainly because cats helped keep venomous snakes at bay and crops free of mice and other vermin, which helped prevent diseases from spreading. Egyptians also appreciated how cats were graceful, protective, loyal and nurturing, yet also aggressive, agile, independent and deadly – all extremely valued traits.

Did you know? The penalty for killing a cat, even by accident, was death!

KITTY SWAG

With a head of a cat and body of a woman, Bastet was honoured with golden jewellery, as cats were associated with riches and royalty.

TAME TABBIES

Egyptians believed cats were magical and brought good luck to the people who looked after them. While worship was saved for Bastet herself, to honour these sacred creatures wealthy families decked them out in precious jewellery and fed them yummy treats.

Mark of respect

According to ancient Greek historian Herodotus, the Egyptians' love for their cats was so great that they shaved off their eyebrows when mourning the death of a family pet.

LIFE AFTER DEATH

When the cats died, they were mummified, often alongside their owners, so they could go to the afterlife together. Mummified cats were also offered up to Bastet in the hope that she'd grant the donor a favour. Many of these mummies were placed in cat-shaped coffins or wrapped in linen, then painted to resemble the animal.

Make your own PROTECTIVE AMULET!

The ancient Egyptians worshipped Bastet and wore jewellery of her to ward off evil spirits. Here's how to make your own protective Bastet-inspired necklace...

You will need:

- Dried macaroni or penne pasta
- Gold and blue/turquoise paint
- Paintbrush
- Craft gems (optional)
- Thin black permanent marker
- Glue gun
- String
- Newspaper

How to do it:

1. Lay out newspaper to protect the surface you're working on. For each amulet, paint 7 pieces of pasta in gold paint and 3 pieces in blue/turquoise paint.

2. When the paint has dried, carefully using a glue gun, glue 4 gold pieces of pasta to each other to make the cat's head. Then glue a blue/turquoise piece to the bottom and continue alternating with gold pieces to make the cat's stripey belly. Wait to dry.

3. With a thin black marker, draw on the cat's triangle ears, eyes, nose and whiskers, as well as any ancient Egyptian-inspired motifs.

4. Channel the Egyptian cats' royal status by jazzing up your amulet with craft gems.

5. Thread some string through the top piece of pasta and loop it around your neck – now you have the spirit of Bastet to protect you wherever you go!

Here comes THE SUN

God of the Sun – Ra – was one of the most important deities in ancient Egypt

Joining forces

Later in Egyptian history, Ra was merged with Amun, who was the god of wind. Together these two powerful deities became a supergod – Amun-Ra – who was so mighty that even the King Tutankhamun was named after him. Translated, his name means 'Living image of Amun'.

SWEATY BEGINNINGS

It's thought that the whole of humankind came into existence from the tears and sweat of Ra – lovely!

Eye will kill you!

According to one myth, Ra lived on the Earth at the beginning of the world, as the king of both gods and humans. As he grew older and weaker, many humans started to lose respect for him. As punishment, Ra sent his Eye to kill those who doubted him. He then left the Earth, leaving Horus – god of the sky – in charge, and travelled across the sky on Nut's back.

Hieroglyphic art of the sun god Ra

SECRET PSEUDONYM

Ra had many names but one in particular was so powerful, whoever used it would be ruler of the entire world and Ra himself. For this reason, it was kept secret from everyone.

Sacred triangle

Ra has loads of origin stories – one such goes that he created himself from a triangular mound of earth before creating all the other gods. The mud's pyramid shape represents the rays of the Sun.

Sons of god

Many pharaohs – or rulers – of Egypt declared that they were descended from Ra, and even added sa Ra, which means 'son of Ra' to their names. The pharaoh Djedefre is thought to be the first to have done this.

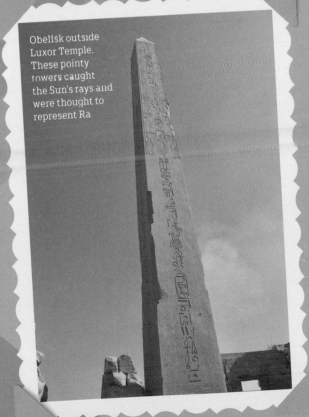

Obelisk outside Luxor Temple. These pointy towers caught the Sun's rays and were thought to represent Ra

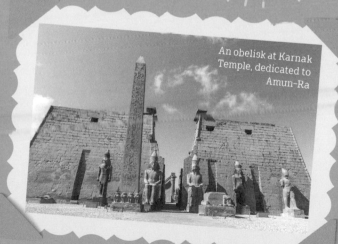

An obelisk at Karnak Temple, dedicated to Amun-Ra

Open-air temples

The Egyptians also built solar temples to honour Ra. These were not built in the usual way – they were open to the sunlight and instead of a statue of the god, they had an obelisk or tower. This was because Ra was represented by the sunlight itself.

MOTHER *of* GODS

Isis was known as the goddess of the moon, life, magic, fertility, motherhood, magic, death, rebirth, protector of women and children and healer of the sick – phew!

At first a relatively unknown goddess, Isis quickly rose in popularity to become one of the most important in ancient Egypt – and is even still revered by some pagans today. Isis is actually her Greek name, her Egyptian name is Aset, meaning 'Queen of the throne'. She was so popular that she had followers through the centuries across ancient Egypt, Greece, Afghanistan and even London.

▲ Throne or a solar disc and cow's horns on her head

THE ULTIMATE JIGSAW

It was thought at one point Isis and her **lover Osiris, who was also her brother,** ruled the world together. They were the offspring of god of the earth Geb and goddess of the sky Nut.

At the peak of his power, **Osiris was murdered and** dismembered by his jealous younger brother Set, who **scattered his body** all over the world. Isis was so sad that she set out to **collect all the pieces** of her brother to put him back together. This is why Isis was thought to have the power to revive the dead. As Osiris comes back to life, instead of being in charge of the living, he becomes **god of the dead and afterlife**.

After Isis brought Osiris back, she **gave birth to a son, Horus,** who grew up to overthrow Set, restoring order back to the world. For this reason, Horus is thought of as the **protector of the ruler of Egypt.**

Egyptians believed that worshipping Isis would ensure their rebirth after death ▼

ANKH

Key of life or key of the Nile that symbolises eternal life. Often held by gods or pharaohs to depict their immortality.

what ARE THE GODS HOLDING?

WAS-SCEPTRE

A long staff with two prongs at the bottom and the head of an animal at the top, this was one of the most important symbols from ancient Egypt. It signified divine power and authority and was carried around by pharaohs, priests, gods and goddesses.

CROOK AND FLAIL

Originally depicting Osiris, these two symbols later came to show a pharaoh's authority. The crook stands for kingship and the flail for the fertility of the land.

DEAD P☠WERFUL

With the head of a dog and the body of a man, Anubis was a fearsome looking god – just as well as he's the god of death, mummification, the afterlife, cemeteries, funeral rites, tombs and the underworld

Weigh to the heart

Ancient Egyptians believed that after death, a person's fate was decided by Anubis, who weighed the hearts of the deceased. If their heart was lighter than the feather of truth, they had lived a good life and could go on to meet Osiris, ruler of the dead, in the afterlife. However, if the heart weighed heavier than the feather, it would be eaten by the fierce demoness Ammut – who had the head of a crocodile, the body of a leopard and the backside of a hippopotamus.

Did you know?

After Set killed Osiris and scattered his body far and wide, Anubis helped Isis to rebuild his body by overseeing the first mummification process.

GAME OF DEATH

The passage to the afterlife depended on your status in life, how much you sinned and what the living did to your body. Want to find out how you'd fare in ancient Egypt?

OH NO YOU'VE BEEN BITTEN BY A MOSQUITO, CAUGHT MALARIA AND DIED!

WERE YOU A..?

COMMON PERSON ...... OR ...... PHARAOH

COMMON PERSON

You've given your relatives the important job of mummifying your body to ensure safe passage to the afterlife. **Do they...?**

Include magic spells from the Book of the Dead. **OR** Decapitate you.

Congratulations! Your body has been mummified and the magic spells included in your coffin give you instructions on how to reach the afterlife. You go to the Hall of Maat, where you are ready to be judged by Anubis. Your first task is to address each of the 42 Assessors of Maat by name, while reciting the sins you did not commit during your lifetime. **Do you...?**

You had disobeyed the king in your life, so your body was killed 'twice' and you will not reach the afterlife, sorry!

Admit to blasphemy. **OR** Say you have no sins.

Your soul is not pure enough to go into the afterlife, sorry!

It's time for Anubis to weigh your heart against the feather of Maat to check you're not lying. **Is your heart...?**

PHARAOH

Lucky you! Only you are allowed to ride by boat to the underworld. **Did your people construct a variety of model boats and bury them alongside you in your pyramid?**

Yes. **OR** No.

Woo! You're on your way to the Hall of Judgment, travelling by solar barge. You have to battle serpents armed with long knives, fire-spitting dragons and five-headed hungry reptiles. You finally get there and see Anubis, who weighs your heart. **Is it...?**

You don't have any transport to get to the afterlife, sorry!

YUM!

AMMUT

HEAVIER THAN THE FEATHER **OR** LIGHTER THAN THE FEATHER

YOU LIED AND YOU HAVE SINNED IN YOUR LIFETIME!
Your heart is eaten by Ammut and you fade into nothingness, sorry!

YOUR RECORD IS SQUEAKY CLEAN
You're permitted to join Osiris in the afterlife, congratulations! You reach paradise and are then reborn as a **ROYAL CAT** of the king.

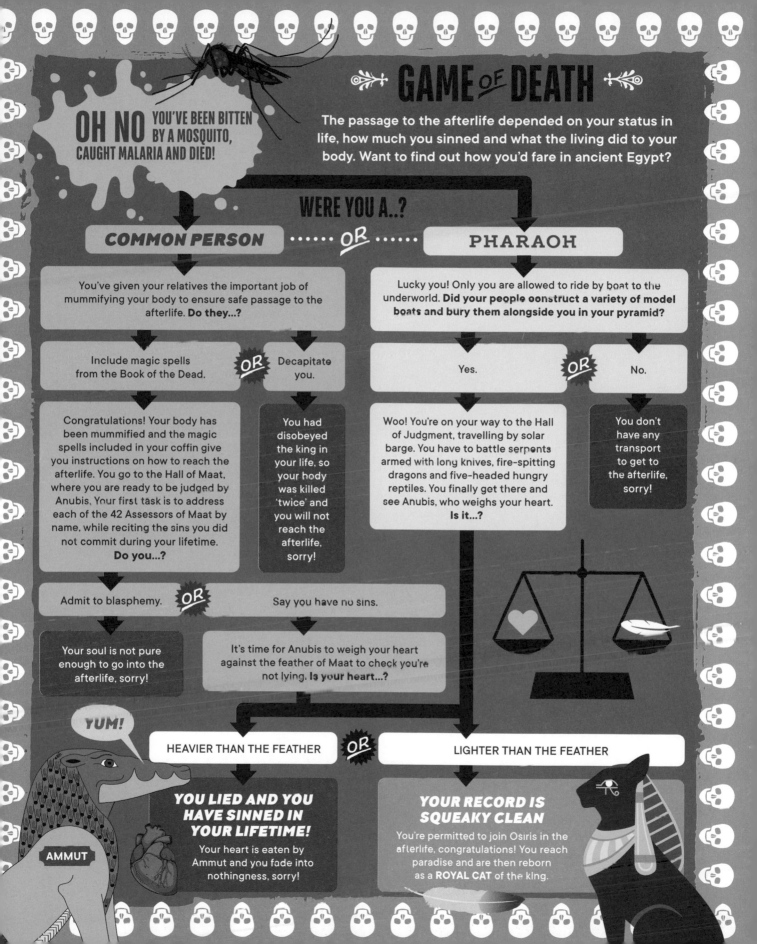

THE EGYPTIAN
BOOK OF THE DEAD

Welcome to the afterlife! Death wasn't the end of the road for the ancient Egyptians. They believed anyone could live forever...

Live forever

The Egyptian Book of the Dead holds the secrets of what Egyptians expected after life. These spells were written from 1500 BC over the course of 1,000 years and were designed to protect people as they journeyed into the unknown. Ancient Egyptian priests called the underworld the Duat. Its hieroglyph is a star in a circle. Karl Richard Lepsius unlocked the secrets of the Book of the Dead in 1842. The historian revealed that hieroglyphs in tombs actually worked as maps for fallen pharaohs to guide them safely in the afterlife. Lepsius' careful ordering of these spells became the Book of the Dead we know today.

▲ Duat hieroglyph

Eye in the sky
Be a space archaeologist and find Saqqara online! Search for the Pyramids of Giza in Maps and see if you can spot any secrets!

1888 IS WHEN THE BOOK OF THE DEAD WAS DISCOVERED
BY EA WALLIS BUDGE

WRITTEN EVERYWHERE

Collecting these ancient passages can't have been easy! Directions for death weren't just chiselled into walls. They have been found written on mummification bandages, tomb trinkets and even on the sarcophagi, the case that Egyptians were laid to rest in! The ancient Egyptians called this curious collection The Chapters of Coming Forth by Day. Why do you think they called it that?

The Chapters of Coming Forth by Day

NEW DISCOVERIES

We're still finding new discoveries about the Egyptian afterlife! Recently, the funerary temple of Queen Nearit was unearthed by Egyptologist Dr Zahi Hawass. It raises questions about the many other mysteries we're yet to discover. If you grew up to be an Egyptologist, what would you want to find out about their way of life?

Mummy MANIA

The ancient Egyptians believed in life after death, making grand coffins and burial tombs for the dead, and preserving their bodies forever... as mummies!

DEAD IMPORTANT

Egyptians thought that when a living being died, their ba (personality or soul) and ka (life force) left the body. It was only through rituals, or burial traditions, that they could be brought back together, allowing the dead to become a blessed spirit, or akh, and achieve immortality, meaning they would live forever in the afterlife.

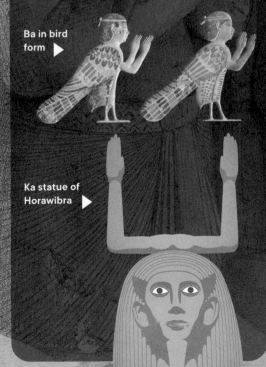

Ba in bird form ▶

Ka statue of Horawibra ▶

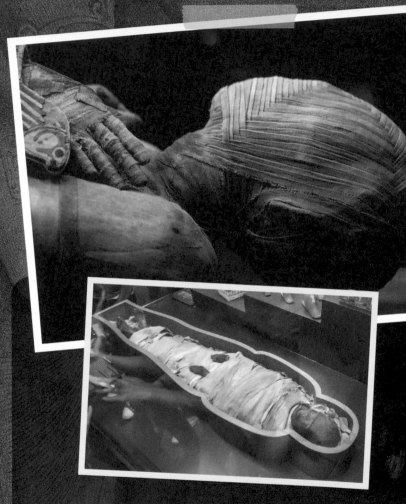

WE ALL NEED SOME BODY

After we die, our bodies naturally begin to rot and decay, which is known as autolysis or decomposition. For people to keep on living in the afterlife, Egyptians believed they would need a body, or khat, that would also be everlasting, so they preserved the dead bodies using a complicated process known as mummification.

WHO'S WHO?

Mummies were laid to rest inside a coffin, known as a sarcophagus, which was sometimes put inside other coffin layers, called a nest. The face of the dead person was painted on the front, so that the spirit could find its way to the right body after death.

SHOW ME THE MONEY, MUMMY

Preserving a dead person for eternity as a mummy was a complicated and costly business, so it was mainly rich people like the pharaohs and other nobles who were buried in this way.

MUMMIES AROUND THE WORLD

BEST PRESERVED

CHINA

The body of Xin Zhui, also known as Lady Dai, was discovered in Hunan in 1968. This noble woman from the Han Dynasty – a family which ruled China for a period of time – was buried inside four coffins over 2,000 years ago. Over 1,000 treasures were also found inside her vast tomb, and she is one of the best-preserved mummies in the world.

WORLD'S OLDEST

DESTROYED

CHILE

The world's oldest mummies were buried 2,000 years before the famous pharaohs of Egypt. The Chinchorro people of northern Chile mummified their dead over 7,000 years ago, while other bodies which were naturally preserved in the dry earth of Chile's Atacama Desert date back 9,000 years.

CANARY ISLANDS

The Guanches people who lived on this group of islands near Africa used clever techniques to preserve people who had died, and buried them in caves. Sadly after Spanish explorers arrived on the islands in the 14th century, they destroyed thousands of mummies and stole the treasures from their tombs.

How to make a MUMMY

Preparing a body for the afterlife took a long time – 70 days! Here's how the ancient Egyptians did it...

1 First the body was thoroughly washed in water and salt.

2 The brain and all the interior organs, except the heart (believed to be the source of good and evil), were removed.

— BRAIN

— LIVER

— LUNGS

— HEART

— STOMACH

— SMALL INTESTINE

— COLON

3 The body was covered in a type of salt called natron – a mix of soda ash and baking soda – for 40 days, to absorb the moisture from the corpse.

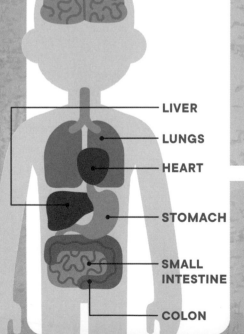

x40 DAYS

NATRON

4 To help keep its human shape, it was stuffed with linen or sand.

5 Make-up, a wig, false eyes and jewellery were added to the body, along with lucky charms, known as amulets, which would protect the dead.

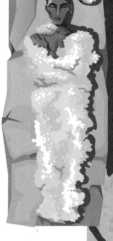

DID YOU KNOW?

If the conditions are right, bodies can be preserved in ice, peat bogs or deserts for many years. This is called natural mummification. When the Egyptian archaeological site of Fag el-Gamous was excavated, it was found to hold thousands of bodies, naturally mummified over 2,000 years ago. Why they were all buried here remains a mystery.

6 The body was treated with herbs, oils and plant resins, then wrapped from head to toe in linen bandages and sealed with more resin, while spells and rituals were performed to ensure their safe journey into the realm of the dead.

7 The body was fitted with a face mask, painted to look like the dead person, and laid in a sarcophagus, or a multiple nest of coffins.

8 The sarcophagus was placed in a tomb, surrounded by the possessions of the dead, and shabtis, small models of slaves or soldiers who would look after them in the afterlife.

JAR JAPES

Removed internal organs, like the liver, stomach, intestines or lungs, were often preserved in natron inside separate containers called canopic jars, and buried in the tomb with the dead. In more recent mummies, the organs were removed, wrapped up and placed back inside the body.

OPERATION MUMMY!

THE CLEVER EGYPTIANS HAD SOME TRICKS FOR REMOVING THE INTERNAL ORGANS FROM INSIDE THE BODY

* Make the brain mushy using a liquid like turpentine, and flush it out through the nose.

* Make a cut on the left side of the body near the stomach and remove the internal organs.

MASTER MUMMIFIER

The mummification process was carried out by an embalmer, who was a priest wearing the mask of Anubis, the jackal-headed god of the dead. Just before burial, they performed an Opening of the Mouth ceremony, believed to give the dead the power of speech, sight and hearing in the afterlife.

Embalming animals

It's not just humans that need a safe trip to the afterlife – in ancient Egypt, even pets got protection!

Gods on Earth

No other culture in history has thought so highly of pets! Ancient Egyptians believed you would be judged on how well you treated animals. It makes sense – they thought they were living versions of the gods.

Wild afterlife

Animals played a huge part in ancient Egyptian life and people believed they had souls just like humans. It wasn't just cats that were held in high regard – mummified birds, crocodiles, dogs, gazelles, monkeys and snakes have also been discovered.

▲ Cat in honour of the goddess Bastet

◀ Young bull

▲ Crocodile as an offering to the god Somek

◀ Gazelle

2,000 DEITIES

EXISTED IN ANCIENT EGYPT

LOOK ALIVE

Many mummies have stayed in incredible condition thanks to the highly-trained holy men that removed their organs. We know that lots of animals had names, thanks to the markings on their graves and in hieroglyphics.

WHEN ANIMALS STARTED GETTING MUMMIFIED

1000 BC

50%
OF HIEROGLYPHS FEATURE ANIMALS

Ibis alliance

Certain species of animals were so common in ancient Egypt that they gained huge groups of followers. One example is the ibis bird, which represented god of wisdom Thoth. The Ibis clan mummified millions of the poor things around 300 BC!

Gifts for the gods

Ancient Egyptians owned pets like we do today, but most mummified animals became offerings. Imagine the souvenirs you buy on holiday today – people could buy wrapped-up beasts and give them as gifts to the gods to get into their good books!

ACTIVITIES

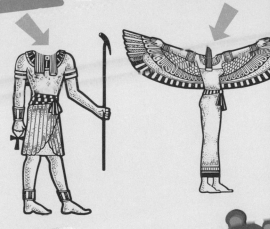

Pet portrait

Got a pet? Draw their head on a human-shaped body and make up your own Egyptian god!

That's a wrap

Get a parent or guardian to help you wrap your favourite cuddly toy in toilet paper. Make it tight with tape.

STAIRWAY TO **HEAVEN**

This blocky build might look basic, but it's the final resting place for royalty to ensure their safe passage to the afterlife – and Djoser is the pyramid that started it all!

DJOSER

FIRST STEPS

Welcome to the world's first-ever pyramid! At least 118 have been labelled pyramids for their pointy tops and tucked-away tombs, but Djoser laid the foundations for what came next. The Step Pyramid started life as a mastaba – one-storey tombs that were flat as a pancake compared to the pyramids.

IMHOTEP
ARCHITECT & PRIEST

THE BEST BUILDER

The Djoser Step Pyramid was designed by Imhotep, one of the most famous ancient Egyptians. It makes sense! He wasn't just an architect... he was a priest for Ra the sun god and a top doctor, too! Over time, Imhotep gained god-like status among Egyptians for being wise.

THE STEP PYRAMID IS

62.5M TALL

THAT'S JUST TALLER THAN **CINDERELLA CASTLE** AT DISNEY WORLD, FLORIDA

View of the Funerary Complex and the Pyramid of Djoser

Inside the Djoser complex

SET IN STONE

Even to the ancient Egyptians, this place was a big deal! The Step Pyramid isn't just one of the oldest pyramids. You're looking at one of the oldest stone building complexes in history.

Named after King Djoser, and built to be his final resting place, his right-hand man Imhotep thought he was so special, he stacked six mastabas on top of each other!

One of the main ways Djoser's is different is that it was built from stone bricks and not mud bricks! Stone's hard (and hard to work with) and this means the royal family had more of a say in how the Step Pyramid took shape.

MADE FOR
KING DJOSER

**NOW LET'S
GO INSIDE**

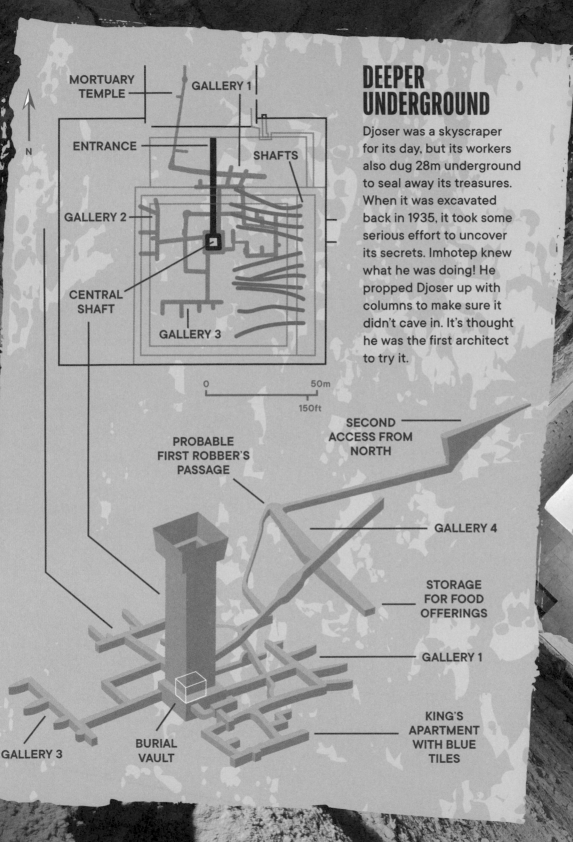

N

MORTUARY
TEMPLE

GALLERY 1

ENTRANCE

SHAFTS

GALLERY 2

CENTRAL
SHAFT

GALLERY 3

0   50m

150ft

DEEPER UNDERGROUND

Djoser was a skyscraper
for its day, but its workers
also dug 28m underground
to seal away its treasures.
When it was excavated
back in 1935, it took some
serious effort to uncover
its secrets. Imhotep knew
what he was doing! He
propped Djoser up with
columns to make sure it
didn't cave in. It's thought
he was the first architect
to try it.

PROBABLE
FIRST ROBBER'S
PASSAGE

SECOND
ACCESS FROM
NORTH

GALLERY 4

STORAGE
FOR FOOD
OFFERINGS

GALLERY 1

KING'S
APARTMENT
WITH BLUE
TILES

GALLERY 3

BURIAL
VAULT

FIT FOR A KING

Djoser was thought to be 'divine of body'... a gift from the gods. An experimental pyramid is only worthy of its ruler and Djoser set the stage for centuries! This army-loving Egyptian king kicked off a new age – which we now call the Old Kingdom.

▲
View of the ancient crypt inside the Step Pyramid of Djoser

3.5
MILES

63

THE PYRAMIDS

5 FAST FACTS

5,000 YEARS

1 The oldest pyramids were being built 5,000 years ago! It's a wonder any of them are still standing today.

2 Ancient Egyptians believed their kings talked to the gods, so they wanted to keep them happy forever.

3 Pyramids' smooth, flat sides supposedly symbolised the Sun. They helped souls get to the afterlife.

4 Everything kings would need in their next life was buried with them. Riches paid for their journey.

5 These pyramids were built for (and named after!) pharoahs Khufu, Khafre and Menkaure, from 2550 to 2490 BC.

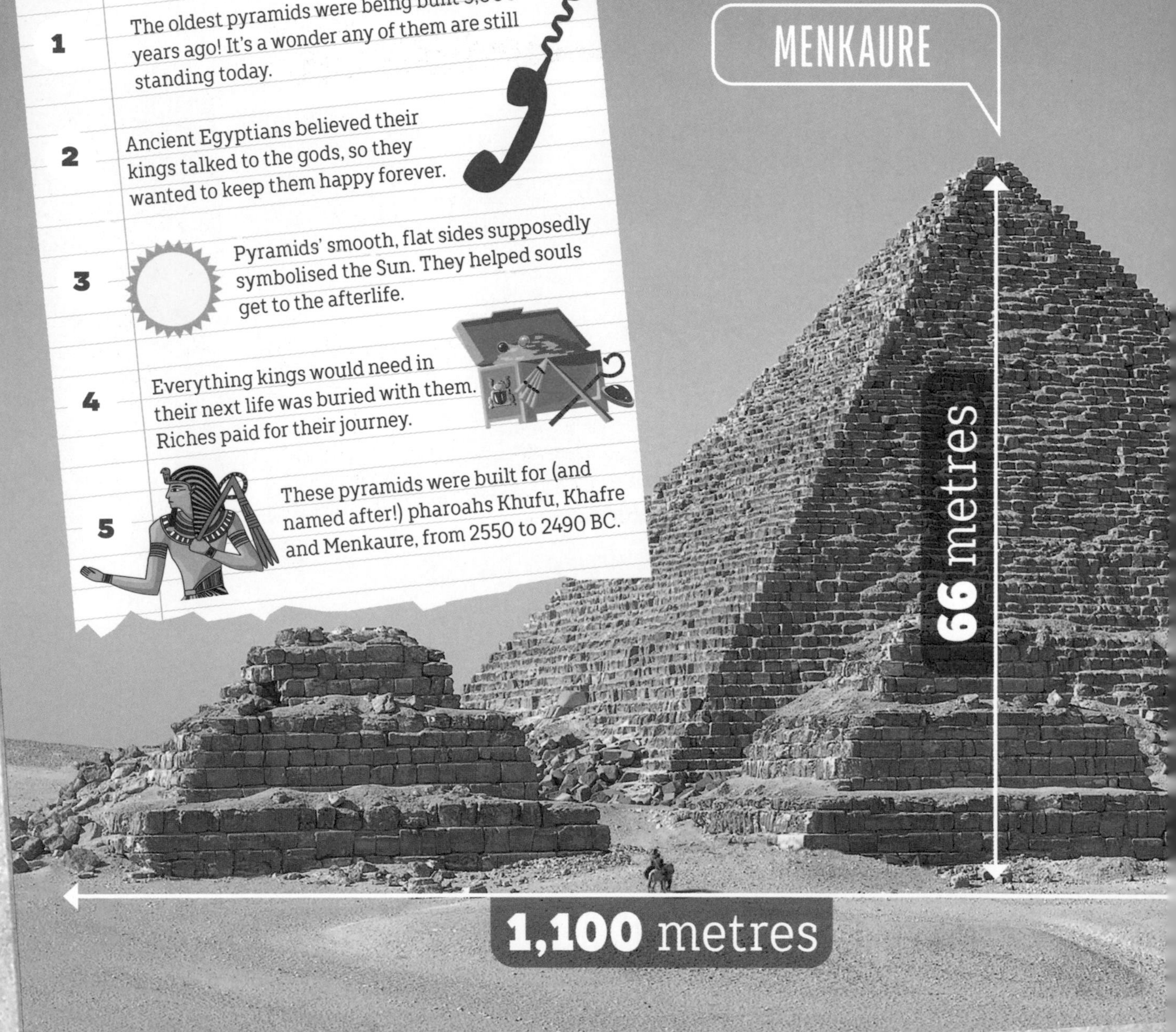

MENKAURE

66 metres

1,100 metres

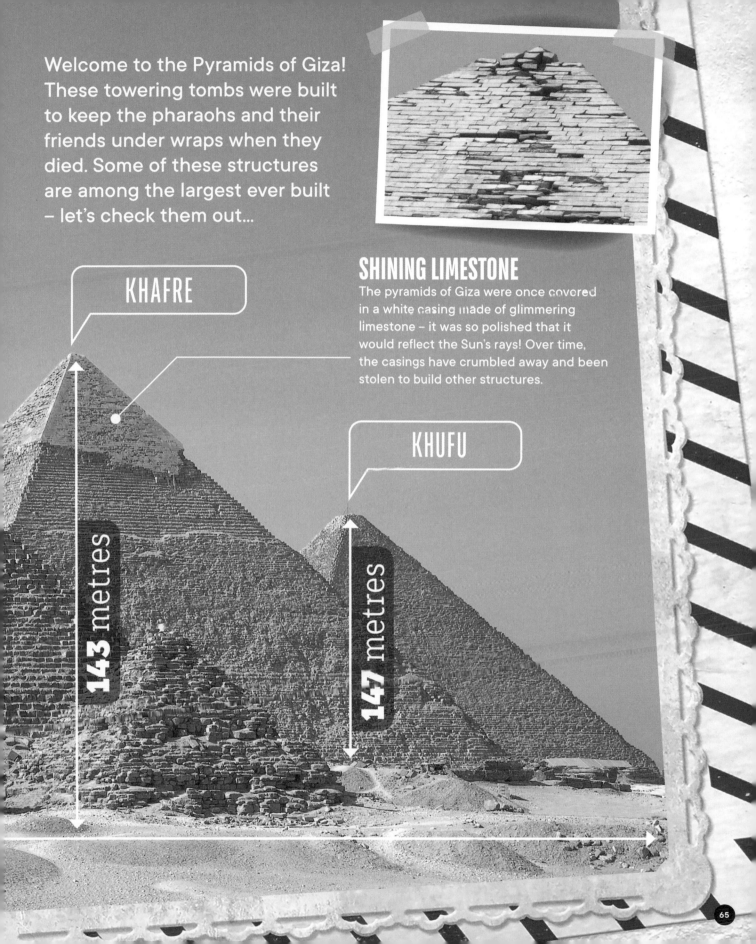

Welcome to the Pyramids of Giza! These towering tombs were built to keep the pharaohs and their friends under wraps when they died. Some of these structures are among the largest ever built – let's check them out...

KHAFRE

SHINING LIMESTONE

The pyramids of Giza were once covered in a white casing made of glimmering limestone – it was so polished that it would reflect the Sun's rays! Over time, the casings have crumbled away and been stolen to build other structures.

KHUFU

143 metres

147 metres

KHUFU

AKA-The Great Pyramid

Khufu is the grandaddy of Giza! It's the oldest of the Seven Wonders of the Ancient World and was the tallest human-made structure on Earth for more than 3,800 years. It's lost some of its shine over the years, but is still standing strong...

HOW MANY **PYRAMIDS** ARE THERE?

118

EIFFEL TOWER

KHUFU

KHAFRE

LONDON EYE

STATUE OF LIBERTY

MENKAURE

THE GREAT PYRAMID TOOK 23 YEARS TO BUILD

LENGTH OF 2x

HEAVY ROCK!

Imagine how hard pyramids were to build! Khufu is made up of 2.3 million blocks of rock and they all weigh about 2.5 tonnes. It took between 20,000 and 100,000 people to build a pyramid, but they wouldn't be able to lift it back up again!

x2.3 MILLION

1.27m

2.5tonnes

0.70m

HOW WERE THEY MADE?

We now know pyramids were heavy and huge, but how were they built? Archaeologists have been arguing about it for almost as long as they've been around! While modern buildings can go up in months, these monstrous monuments took decades!

MOVING MOUNTAINS

The biggest argument over how the pyramids were built is about how workers moved the stone blocks around. It can be easy to imagine how we might make them with modern technology but ancient Egyptians didn't have the tools of today.

SKILLED BUILDERS

For years it was believed that slaves did all the hard work, but building pyramids called for mental strength and not just muscles! The pyramids were built to honour Egypt's rulers so it's likely that they hired the very best men for the job.

BETTER WITH TIME

The pyramids were built over long periods of time as the Egyptians wanted to make life easier! Khufu became a brilliant blueprint for Khafre, the pyramid built for his son. Designers and managers learned new tricks too.

STILL STANDING STRONG

It's likely that not even the ancient Egyptians could have imagined how long their sharp-topped structures would stay standing for. Think about a modern city like London – how long do you think today's skyscrapers could stay up?

An ancient PYRAMID

PYRAMID'S POINT

Thousands of years ago, shiny, polished limestone made the pyramids glow. Dug from limestone quarries 15km down the Nile, Giza's cap once looked out of this world.

Ready for an adventure? Grab your explorer's hat and take a step inside an ancient pyramid! We're going in...

THE KING'S CHAMBER

The ruler was always the centre of attention. Many pyramids made the most of the natural world, laying flat or even being built into mountains. Not Khufu though – his chamber is raised up.

Scientists have found a huge void in Khufu's pyramid using high-tech scanners. They are still not sure if it is a cave-in... or a smart way to cut down on how much stone was used.

TOMBS TOGETHER

The rulers didn't rest alone... or did they? Years ago, explorers called this less impressive tomb the queen's chamber. By the time modern Egyptologists found Khufu's second chamber, it had been stripped bare. Maybe he needed two rooms for all his treasure?

x23

THAT'S HOW TALL KHUFU'S PYRAMID IS... IF YOU STACK GIRAFFES ON TOP OF EACH OTHER!

Almost all pyramids were built to the west of the Nile, to satisfy Osiris. As the Sun sets to the west, the ancient Egyptians thought building there would help them reach the afterlife.

TUCKED AWAY

Deep under the pyramids, you'll find a hidden tomb. Even today, archaeologists are finding tunnels that link the legends of the old world together. British explorer Andrew Collins recently found rare species of bats and venomous spiders in its depths.

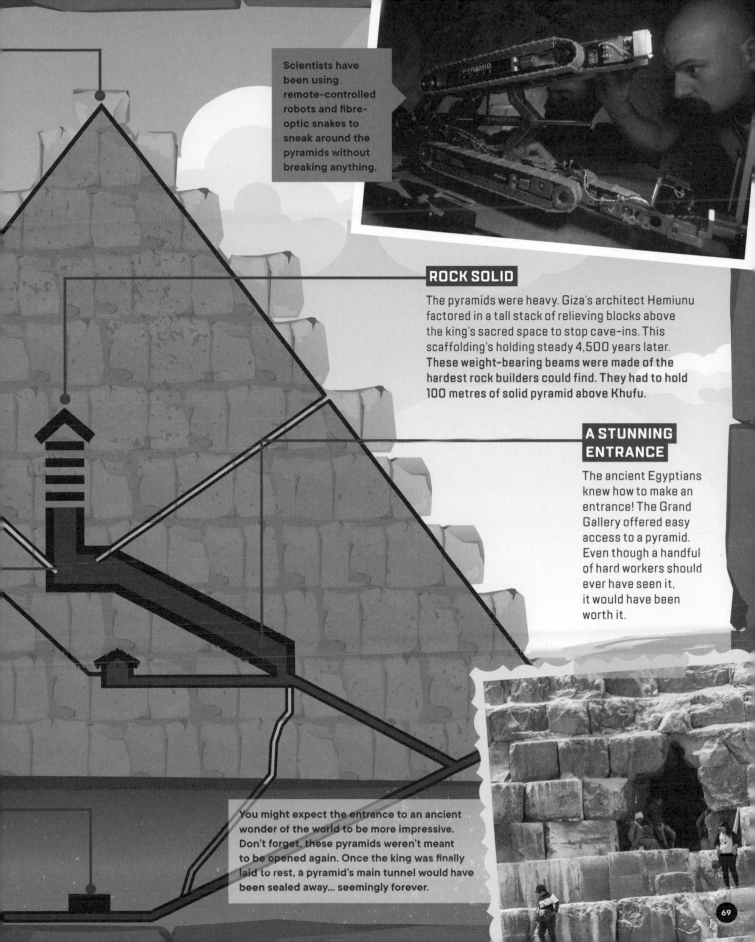

ROCK SOLID

The pyramids were heavy. Giza's architect Hemiunu factored in a tall stack of relieving blocks above the king's sacred space to stop cave-ins. This scaffolding's holding steady 4,500 years later. These weight-bearing beams were made of the hardest rock builders could find. They had to hold 100 metres of solid pyramid above Khufu.

A STUNNING ENTRANCE

The ancient Egyptians knew how to make an entrance! The Grand Gallery offered easy access to a pyramid. Even though a handful of hard workers should ever have seen it, it would have been worth it.

You might expect the entrance to an ancient wonder of the world to be more impressive. Don't forget, these pyramids weren't meant to be opened again. Once the king was finally laid to rest, a pyramid's main tunnel would have been sealed away... seemingly forever.

ENTER THE VALLEY OF THE KINGS

Who would have thought that one of Egypt's most spectacular and popular destinations would be... a massive cemetery?

WORST-KEPT SECRET

Pharaohs used to build great pyramids to be buried in before they realised they were far too obvious targets for tomb robbers. So instead, they carved tombs into desert rocks, deep beneath mountains in a lonely valley for greater protection... Or that's what they thought!

ROYAL RESTING PLACE

The Valley of the Kings is a royal burial ground for pharaohs from the New Kingdom – from around 1500–1000 BC. This was the golden age of the civilisation of ancient Egypt, when the country was at its richest and most powerful.

Did you know?

This new burial tradition started with **Thutmose I**, the first king to have an 'invisible' tomb in the Valley. It's thought royal architect Ineni would use foreign captives to build tombs... and then kill them so no one could know about the place!

TOP 3 OF THE BEST TOMBS

IMAGINE: you enter a narrow and dark staircase, descend the main corridor and prepare yourself to discover the most fascinating scenes – with walls and ceiling covered with colourful paintings that were meant only to be seen by the Egyptian gods!

BRONZE MEDAL

LARGEST

was actually not built for a pharaoh but for the sons of Ramesses II. Originally dismissed as being insignificant, further exploration in recent years revealed that it contained at least 130 rooms!

SILVER MEDAL

LONGEST

belonged to Queen Hatshepsut. It was originally constructed for Thutmose I and then adapted by his daughter to accommodate them both. Her burial chamber is about 215 metres from the entrance and 100 metres below the surface.

GOLD MEDAL

BEST-DECORATED

is Seti I's, with its walls filled with beautifully preserved images (at the time of discovery) from many ancient texts. As well as a painting of the night sky with all Egyptian constellations covering the ceiling of the burial chamber.

TRUST NO ONE!

Most of the tombs were looted within 100 years of being sealed, but you may be surprised by who the robbers were. A mix of slaves, priests who participated in the burial ritual and even royalty robbing their own ancestors! Stealing their possessions was one thing, but more importantly, if the preserved body got seriously damaged or the nameplate on vandalised coffins became unreadable, then the dead would be lost forever – and could no longer reach the afterlife.

A NEVER-ENDING EXCAVATION

By the early 20th century, over 60 tombs had been discovered, but even with their entrances extremely well hidden, most of these had already been opened and looted thousands of years ago! Only one had remained (almost) intact until modern times, making it the most famous of them all: Tutankhamun's tomb. And with more buried entrances discovered in recent years, experts believe that the Valley still hides many more treasures to uncover...

GIANT
guardian

A sphinx or sphynx is a mythical creature which has the body of a lion and the head of a human – often of a pharaoh or god. Whilst also an important figure in Greek mythology, which is where the term sphinx comes from, for the ancient Egyptians the sphinx was a spiritual guardian and protector of important areas such as tombs and temples...

Face off
The head of the Great Sphinx is thought to be modelled after the Pharaoh Khafra, but over the years its features have eroded. The statue used to have a long, braided beard and a nose. The original version would have looked a lot different to what we can see now – evidence suggests that the face and body were painted red, the beard was blue and the headdress was yellow.

THE GREAT SPHINX OF GIZA IS ONE OF THE WORLD'S LARGEST STATUES AT

20 METRES (66FT) HIGH

AND A HUGE

73 METRES (240FT) LONG

THAT'S THE LENGTH OF ABOUT **16 CARS!**

What is the Great Sphinx sitting on?
Legend has it that underneath lies a Hall of Records, which contains information about alchemy, astronomy, mathematics, magic, medicine and more. As it's very delicate, however, it's forbidden to excavate under the giant structure, so no such library of knowledge has ever been found.

MYSTERIOUS BEGINNINGS

No one knows when exactly or how the Great Sphinx was created, but it's thought to be around **4,500 YEARS OLD** and would have needed **100 PEOPLE** to carve the statue out of a single mass of limestone over **THREE YEARS.**

UNFINISHED BUSINESS

There's evidence that workers on the Great Sphinx left the unfinished statue in a hurry – archaeologists have found what appears to be remnants of a workman's lunch and tool kit.

How do you use an ancient Egyptian doorbell?
Toot-and-come-in!

SNIFFING OUT THE UNKNOWN

The Great Sphinx's nose has been missing for centuries and there are a few theories of where it went. Some believe French military leader Napoleon fired it off with a cannonball around the end of the 18th century. Others say there's evidence that points to the nose being missing from before Napoleon's time and that it was more likely vandalised sometime in the 13th century. No one really *nose* for sure though!

CHAPTER 3
DISCOVERING EGYPT

Just how do we know so much about the ancient world of the Egyptians? Thanks to the work and discoveries of archaeologists, historians and Egyptologists, the truth about this civilisation has been pieced together. Read on to find out how hieroglyphics were cracked and the story of how Tutankhamun was uncovered. You'll also get the chance to meet a few of Egypt's most amazing animals...

HOW DO WE KNOW SO MUCH?

The reason we have a lot of information about people who lived thousands of years ago is because of archaeology. But what exactly is it?

Mysteries of human history

There are no written records for most of human history, so we need to look at ruins and objects (artefacts) left behind a long time ago to be able to understand how people lived in ancient times. Put simply, archaeology is a lot about looking into old things! This is the job of archaeologists, half-scientists and half-detectives, who dig into the earth – and the past – to find clues and reconstruct a picture of lost civilisations.

Digging up dirt

Before digging can even start, archaeologists create a precise map of the excavation site so they can later keep detailed records of their findings. This is because digging also means destroying, and the original composition of the site that remained intact for hundreds or thousands of years is then lost forever. Once the excavation is complete, they can send newly discovered artefacts to the lab to be analysed... and unravel secrets of the past.

EGYPTOLOGY PIONEERS

Because of the vast knowledge they need to do their job properly, archaeologists focus on a specific time and region, or develop expertise on a particular issue. A specialist in ancient Egypt is called an Egyptologist. Here are two iconic examples:

NAME: Mary Brodrick
(British, 1858-1933)

ACHIEVEMENT: One of the first British women to undertake excavations in Egypt.

KEY FEATURE: *Determination.* Mary went against all, including her own teacher and other students playing tricks on her, to study in a male-dominated subject at the time. She became a renowned expert giving lectures at the British museum.

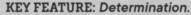

NAME: Selim Hassan
(Egyptian, 1886–1961)

ACHIEVEMENT: One of the first to proclaim Egypt's right to have its stolen antiquities returned.

KEY FEATURE: *Passion.* As well as supervising the excavation of many tombs, Selim spent much of his life writing the complete *Encyclopedia of Ancient Egypt.* It is now considered the most important and influential reference book on ancient Egyptian history.

HOW LUCKY IS THAT?
Accidental discoveries around the world

The Venus de Milo

WHERE: Greece
WHEN: 1820
WHO: A farmer removing some stones from a crumbling wall to use for his farm.
WHAT: An ancient Greek statue depicting the Greek goddess of love and beauty, Aphrodite.
WOW-FACTOR: It is considered by many as the most beautiful sculpture in the world, but weirdly enough, it is her missing arms that are her most famous feature!

Lascaux Cave paintings

WHERE: France
WHEN: 1940
WHO: A teenager following his dog that fell down a hole.
WHAT: A cave covered with 15,000-year-old paintings.
WOW-FACTOR: Its walls are decorated with about 600 painted and drawn animals and nearly 1,500 engravings!

Terracotta Army

WHERE: China
WHEN: 1974
WHO: Farmers digging a well to find underground water.
WHAT: A massive burial tomb built for Qin Shi Huang, the first emperor of China, dating to around 210 BC, over 2,000 years ago.
WOW-FACTOR: There are over 8,000 life-sized statues of soldiers buried along with the emperor!

Survival of the fittest

Most things decay over time, but it all depends on the environment they are left in and the material they are made of. So, textiles (clothes) decompose rather easily compared to clay (pottery) or metal (coins). And wood (some weapons and tools) lasts much longer in the desert than in the rainforest. This is due to the absence of water, providing excellent conditions for preservation.

Discovering the
BOY KING

When archaeologists stumbled across King Tutankhamun's tomb, they found much more than expected...

Archaeologist Howard Carter was hired by wealthy English aristocrat Lord Carnarvon, an enthusiastic amateur Egyptologist, to find Tutankhamun's tomb. Even though many archaeologists were convinced all the best tombs had been found already, Carter and Carnarvon were determined. So once they got permission to dig the Valley of the Kings in 1914, the search was on...

After many fruitless years and the First World War suspending the dig, Carnarvon's patience and money started to run out – Carter only had one more chance! But this was all he needed: while excavating the very last plot in November 1922, he found – by accident – the first step leading to a promising doorway... and to Tutankhamun's tomb!

ENTRANCE TO TUTANKHAMUN'S TOMB !!

HOWARD CARTER, ARCHAEOLOGIST !

A simple affair

Untouched for more than 3,000 years, the tomb was the smallest royal one of the Valley of the Kings – far too cosy for a pharaoh. It's thought to have been built for somebody else, but was used for King Tut instead when he died unexpectedly at a young age. The reason it wasn't found for so long is because it got overlooked and buried by debris from later tombs. In fact, the tomb of Ramesses VI was built almost on top of it!

Although many have suspected until recent years there were hidden rooms, the tomb consists of just four. The first was so crammed with royal possessions that it took months to remove them all before Carter could finally reach the burial chamber. Imagine his excitement when he realised the next door had remained sealed, which meant that nobody else before him – not even robbers – had reached that far…

The greatest treasure of them all

Discovering thousands of priceless artefacts is one thing, but what was lying in the burial chamber would surpass everything. However, this final step would be a very long and difficult operation. The entire chamber was occupied by four shrines – large, stunning but fragile containers with a sarcophagus inside. Imagine lifting the very heavy broken lid, especially in such a confined space! Then, opening delicately not one, but three coffins inside each other, before revealing the most valuable of all the treasures: the perfectly preserved mummy adorned with a majestic gold mask.

IT TOOK HOWARD 7 YEARS searching the Valley before he found it

TUT'S TOMB TREASURES

It took Carter almost 10 years to catalogue more than 5,000 items, from statues to jewellery, musical instruments to weapons, but also chariots and model boats. And Tutankhamun was a minor king, so imagine the full treasures of major pharaohs with much bigger tombs!

CANOPIC JARS
Containing all the king's organs – ew!

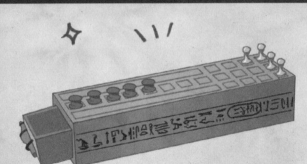

SENET
Fun boardgame that also symbolised the passage of life after death.

PERSONAL FAN
Elaborate, gold fan to keep cool in the afterlife.

THROWING STICKS
Used to hunt birds, these were for successful hunting in the afterlife.

10 YEARS
TO CATALOGUE

GO FOR GOLD

Even 3,300 years ago, Tutankhamun had his very own supercar! Kings' chariots had some serious horsepower – they were pulled by actual horses! This gold chariot may just have been for show, but scientists have marvelled at its speedy design.

Picture Postcard featuring sun view with beautiful sunset photo by E. Müller

AIR MAIL

16 CENTS 16

FOR CORRESPONDENCE   FOR ADDRESS ONLY

LINEN GLOVES
Thought to have been used by the king himself when he went on his chariot in the wintertime.

BLING!
All sorts of exciting jewellery for King Tut to look fabulous in the afterlife, such as anklets, buckles, bracelets, chest adornments, necklaces, collars and earrings.

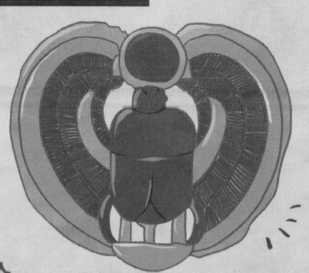

A TOTAL OF **5,398 OBJECTS** WERE FOUND IN THE TOMB

THE CURSE OF
King Tut's tomb

It is believed that anyone who should disturb a mummy or a pharaoh's tomb will be cursed – bringing bad luck, illness or even death... So was something terrible unleashed when King Tut's tomb was opened?

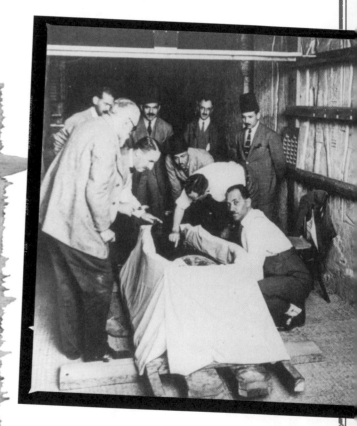

Media frenzy

The tomb's discovery and mysteries captivated imaginations thanks to extensive press coverage. The sleepy Valley of the Kings suddenly became swamped by visitors and reporters from around the world, and there was a fierce competition to report the story. As only one newspaper had exclusive access, the rest of the press started to make up their own stories, publishing gossip rather than facts. Their favourite subject? The curse of Tutankhamun.

It all started with a bird...

When Carter's pet canary was killed by a snake, some interpreted it as something more because his house had been broken into by a royal cobra, the symbol of Egyptian monarchy, also worn on Tutankhamun's head. This could have been dismissed as a coincidence, if it wasn't for the fact it happened on the day Carter opened Tutankhamun's tomb! The story fuelled local rumours of a curse, but nothing more, until less than two months later – when Carnarvon died.

Tut May Have Sent Spirit to Kill His Finder, Doyle Says

HOW BIZARRE?!

Carnarvon's death was caused by... a mosquito bite. It became infected, and he eventually died of blood poisoning. At the exact moment of his death, it was reported that all the lights in Cairo mysteriously went out, and his dog back in England let out a howl and dropped dead that same night!

Fake news

This time, the story made headlines all over the world, thanks to none other than *Sherlock Holmes* author Sir Arthur Conan Doyle, who attributed his death to 'malevolent spirits'. Although his obsession with the supernatural was known to all – the man believed in fairies – his declaration did the trick. Even Italian dictator Benito Mussolini, who had recently accepted an Egyptian mummy as a gift, demanded it be removed from Rome straightaway!

So, curse or no curse?

Carter didn't believe in any of it, calling these unfortunate events 'foolish superstitions'. However, the press claimed many people associated with the tomb opening soon died under mysterious circumstances – so the idea of a curse would persist, even today. But there are logical explanations, the most widely accepted one being that people fell ill from breathing in poisonous moulds and bacteria that flourished in the sealed space for thousands of years.

ORIGIN OF A MYTH:

THE MUMMY RETURNS

The legend of the mummy's curse actually started way before King Tut's tomb discovery. Believe it or not, 'unrolling mummies' were popular shows in Victorian Britain. Wealthy people would buy an Egyptian mummy and open the bandages in front of a fascinated audience – for science purposes as much as for entertainment. And this, at a time when it was considered rude not to go out without wearing gloves! It is believed such spectacles inspired the first writers to create scary stories of the vengeful mummy coming back to life.

TUTMANIA

If Carnarvon and Carter attained instant celebrity status, the world went absolutely mad for Tutankhamun. There was a craze for anything to do with ancient Egypt in the 1920s, inspiring fashion, architecture and music. Even then-US President Hoover named one of his dogs King Tut!

FEEBLE PHARAOH

Thanks to his famous tomb and its supposed curse, much is known about King Tutankhamun after death – but what was he like in life?

Daddy not-so cool

His dad, Akhenaten, was nicknamed the Heretic King because of all the radical changes he brought in – mainly declaring that only one god (Aten) was to be worshipped and erasing all records of the other gods favoured by ancient Egypt. This didn't go down well with the majority of people and after King Tut came to the throne – aged nine – he spent much of his reign undoing his dad's mess.

Always under the weather

He may be the most famous pharaoh, but he's certainly not the greatest. He was a frail, weak boy with loads of ailments, such as a bone abnormality called necrosis (when the tissue dies), scoliosis, a club foot and other genetic deformities thought to have come from inbreeding.

DID YOU KNOW? King Tut's dodgy foot and bones meant he needed assistance to walk – 130 used canes were found buried along with him. He's also the only known pharaoh depicted sitting down when doing physical activities such as archery.

HOW DID HE DIE?

The Boy King sadly only made it to age 19. Thanks to modern tech and DNA tests, there are loads of theories behind his death, but the jury's still out on what might have finished him off. Here are some of the most common theories – what do you think it was?

TOOTH INFECTION

His skull had an impacted wisdom tooth but there isn't much evidence of an infection.

Unlikely

FELL OFF AND RUN OVER BY CHARIOT

Severe trauma to the left torso and side – might a fall have broken his legs and pelvis, leading to infection and blood poisoning?

For ages this was the main theory, it even had a dedicated BBC documentary, but further analysis has made it *Unlikely*

BRUTALLY MURDERED

Researchers thought that damage to the skull was proof that King Tut was hit over the head and murdered by his rivals in cold blood.

Unlikely

The damage is now thought to be from when the body was moved.

GANGRENE FOLLOWING LEG FRACTURE

Scans have shown that the king broke his leg just before he died – could this have become infected and gangrenous, leading to his death?

Likely

MALARIA

A disease common to the Nile, tests have shown King Tut to have caught several strains over his life – perhaps one of them topped him off?

Likely

MARFAN SYNDROME

A genetic disorder that causes a long head, curved spine and fused spine – all things that King Tut's mummy had.

Unlikely

Further tests disproved this.

EPILEPSY

Some evidence that he may have died from a seizure.

Fairly likely

BITTEN BY A HIPPOPOTAMUS

He was mummified without his heart and chest wall – could a hippo's bite have torn them out?

Unlikely

Sound it out

Unfortunately for us, we don't know how so many hieroglyphs sounded. Today we have vowels to signal sounds but the ancient Egyptians assumed a lot.

Learn a language

Hieroglyphs were complicated. Official scribes were trained to read, write and even make up new words. And while grammar is such a big part of how we understand language today, these ancient marks didn't even have punctuation. But despite this difficult job, you would have wanted to be a hieroglyph scribe. They were so important that they wouldn't be sent to war.

▶ 1968 postage stamp shows a sculpture of a scribe

EGYPTIAN ART

POSTAGE
65
DIRHAM
SHARJAH
& DEPENDENCIES
الشارقة وملحقاتها

THE ROSETTA STONE

This rock is the gateway to understanding everything about ancient Egypt!

Codebreakers

This huge chunk of basalt rock is so useful because it has the same text in different languages and styles next to each other. Imagine how easy this made translating it between ancient images and letters. You can see the Rosetta Stone yourself at the British Museum.

◀ Fragment of Roman mosaic of Alexander the Great (100 BC)

Speaking Greek

Greek invaders couldn't read or write in hieroglyphs when Alexander the Great invaded ancient Egypt in 332 BC. This put them at odds with the people of Egypt straight away.

War of the words

The Rosetta Stone isn't the only translation key of its kind. It's special because it was designed by Pharaoh Ptolemy V so everyone would understand signs saying he was the rightful king.

Read all about it

The Rosetta Stone is named after the town where it was found by the Nile. A French captain called Pierre-François Bouchard discovered it while building a fort in 1799.

SEE IT AT THE BRITISH MUSEUM IN LONDON

Welcome to WILD EGYPT!

Some incredible critters roam around Egypt's deserts and wild places. Here are some top ones to spot...

NILE CROCODILE

Growing up to a whopping five metres long and weighing up to 750kg, these awesome reptiles can be found across the African continent, and rule the Nile. With their thick, armour-like skin, these tough cookies are at the top of the food chain, snapping up fish, birds and antelopes in their strong jaws, bursting out of the depths in blistering attacks. Chomp!

DID YOU KNOW?

Crocodiles have one of the most powerful bites in the animal kingdom, with strong jaws that can break up bones and even tough turtle shells. Their 60 to 110 teeth are replaced with new ones each time their chompers break or fall out.

FENNEC OR DESERT FOX

Easy to identify with its huuuuge, pointy ears, the world's smallest type of fox roams the Sahara Desert, its sandy coloured fur providing camouflage from predators amidst the rolling, golden dunes. They love to munch insects and escape the desert's sizzling heat by digging out tunnels and chilling in cool burrows underground.

Listen up
The ears of the fennec fox can grow up to 15cm long, which can be almost half their entire body length. They enable it to seek out scuttling prey to eat and keep the fox's body temperature down by helping to release excess heat.

CAIRO SPINY MOUSE

Named after Egypt's capital city, this sandy or grey-brown mouse is mostly found in dry stony canyons, scurrying around date palms, or sometimes running around houses! It comes out at night to hunt for food, nibbling on fruits, seeds and insects. Growing up to 18cm long, their tails can be as long as their body, and they have large eyes and ears.

Mummy munchers
Cairo spiny mice have been spotted in Egyptian tombs at Gebel Drunka, munching cheekily on the ancient mummies – yikes!

NUBIAN IBEX

Skipping up steep mountain slopes and teetering on soaring cliffs, these wild mountain goats are extreme rock climbers. They live in herds and descend from higher elevations where they rest at night to graze on grasses during the day, their shiny coats reflecting the strong desert sun and providing a waterproof shield when it rains.

You go, curl friend
The male ibex grows a pair of impressive arching horns which they use in battles with other males over females during the mating season and to defend their territory. They can reach over a metre in length, so never mess with an ibex!

HYRAX

You'll find this curious mammal, which looks like a large guinea pig, hopping around in rocky outcrops across many countries in Africa, and along the banks of the river Nile in Egypt. Excellent climbers, they live in large groups and are herbivores (vegetarian). Listen out for their loud shrieks which they use to warn others when danger's about. Aaarrgghh!

Horsing around
Fossils of prehistoric hyrax dating from 30 million years ago have been found, showing that these ancient ancestors were as big as a modern-day horse!

CARACAL

This athletic and agile predator can leap over three metres into the air to snatch birds mid-flight for dinner. Easily recognised by their distinctive tufty black ears, caracals can grow up to a metre long and live much of their life alone or in pairs, hunting at night and seeking out shade by day. They can growl, spit and hiss, but when content they purr like a kitten.

Cat fact

Ancient Egyptians depicted caracals in their paintings and gilded statues, often showing them as the guardians of royal tombs, and some were even found embalmed in burial chambers.

EGYPTIAN COBRA

These incredible sssssnakes can be found slithering through a wide range of habitats, from farmlands to deserts, and they've even been spotted swimming in the Mediterranean Sea! Like other cobras, it has long ribs that expand to form a hood. Growing to just under three metres long, their deadly venom would kill a fully grown elephant in just three hours!

Snake it up

In Egyptian art, the cobra often represented Wadjet, the powerful daughter of the sun god, Ra. She protected Egypt and the cosmos from chaos. Her symbol of a raised cobra, called a uraeus, was also found on the front of the pharaohs' crowns.

THE BIG
EGYPT QUIZ

Read the issue, then put your newfound knowledge to the test!

1 When did people first settle around the Sahara Desert? (*Turn to p7 for a hint*)

2 What does the word Nile mean in Greek? (*Turn to p9 for a hint*)

3 Which pharaoh commissioned the Great Pyramid at Giza? (*Turn to p11 for a hint*)

4 What is the name for a period of time where a civilisation is ruled by a line of people from the same family group? (*Turn to p15 for a hint*)

5 Which female pharaoh preferred to be portrayed as a man? (*Turn to p16 for a hint*)

6 How long did Ramesses II rule Egypt? (*Turn to p18 for a hint*)

7 What percentage of ancient Egyptians were slaves? (*Turn to p21 for a hint*)

8 Where did doctor priests train in medicine? (*Turn to p23 for a hint*)

9 What was the name of the scales used by ancient Egyptians to weigh goods? (*Turn to p28 for a hint*)

10 After which battle was the world's first peace treaty signed? (*Turn to p33 for a hint*)

11 In what year did Antony and Cleopatra commit suicide? (*Turn to p34 for a hint*)

12 Who was the god of the sky? (*Turn to p40 for a hint*)

13 How did ancient Egyptians mourn the death of a pet cat? (*Turn to p45 for a hint*)

14 Which two gods merged to become Amun-Ra? (*Turn to p46 for a hint*)

15 Who collected the pieces of Osiris and put them back together? (*Turn to p49 for a hint*)

16 Who is the god of death and the underworld? (*Turn to p50 for a hint*)

17 What is the name of the coffin in which a mummy was laid to rest? (*Turn to p55 for a hint*)

18 What was the name of the containers in which a mummy's organs were preserved? (*Turn to p57 for a hint*)

19 What was the world's first-ever pyramid? (*Turn to p60 for a hint*)

20 The pyramids of Giza were once covered in a white casing made of... what? (*Turn to p65 for a hint*)

21 During what period was the Valley of the Kings used as a royal burial ground? (*Turn to p70 for a hint*)

22 Which archaeologist found Tutankhamun's tomb? (*Turn to p78 for a hint*)

23 How old was Tutankhamun when he died? (*Turn to p85 for a hint*)

24 How long can Nile crocodiles grow? (*Turn to p88 for a hint*)

25 How long would it take an Egyptian cobra's venom to kill an elephant? (*Turn to p91 for a hint*)

GLOSSARY

AGRICULTURE
The farming of crops and animals for food and materials like clothing.

AILMENT
An illness.

AMBASSADORS
People who visit another country in order to represent their own and speak on its behalf.

CARCINOGENIC
Something that can cause cancer.

DEITY
A god or goddess.

DISMEMBERED
When a body has its limbs cut off.

DYNASTY
A line of rulers all from the same family.

EGYPTOLOGIST
An archaeologist or historian who specialises in studying ancient Egypt.

EPILEPSY
A common brain condition that can cause seizures.

FERTILITY
Being able to produce children or crops.

HIEROGLYPHS
A writing system composed of pictures representing words or sounds.

HITTITES
An ancient group of people who lived in Anatolia in Western Asia.

IMMORTALITY
To live forever.

IRRIGATION
Using channels to divert water towards crops to help them grow.

MALARIA
A serious disease spread by parasites carried by some mosquitoes. Its symptoms include a high fever and chills.

MALEVOLENT
When someone wishes to do something deliberately harmful to someone else.

MIGRATING
Moving from one place to another.

PROSPERITY
Being wealthy and successful.

PROTOTYPE
Something that is the first of its kind that is later used as a model for making similar things.

RITUALS
Religious ceremonies where a series of meaningful actions are carried out.

SHRINE
A place that is considered holy or sacred because of its connection with a god or person of religious importance.

TREATY
A formal agreement made between two or more states.

TRIBUTARIES
The smaller rivers or streams that flow into a larger river.

QUIZ ANSWERS

1. 9000 BC
2. Great river
3. Khufu
4. Dynasty
5. Hatshepsut
6. 66 years
7. 10%
8. The House of Life
9. Deben
10. The Battle of Kadesh
11. 30 BC
12. Horus
13. By shaving their eyebrows
14. Ra the sun god and Amun the god of wind
15. Isis
16. Anubis
17. Sarcophagus
18. Canopic jars
19. Djoser
20. Limestone
21. New Kingdom
22. Howard Carter
23. 19
24. Up to 5 metres
25. Three hours

Coin count - page 28 & 29

INDEX

First published 2023 by Button Books, an imprint of Guild of Master Craftsman Publications Ltd, Castle Place, 166 High Street, Lewes, East Sussex, BN7 1XU, UK. Copyright in the Work © GMC Publications Ltd, 2023. ISBN 978 1 78708 131 4. Distributed by Publishers Group West in the United States. All rights reserved. No part of this publication may be reproduced, stored in a retrieval system, or transmitted in any form or by any means without the prior permission of the publisher and copyright owner. While every effort has been made to obtain permission from the copyright holders for all material used in this book, the publishers will be pleased to hear from anyone who has not been appropriately acknowledged and to make the correction in future reprints. The publishers and authors can accept no legal responsibility for any consequences arising from the application of information, advice, or instructions given in this publication. A catalogue record for this book is available from the British Library. Editorial: Samhita Foria, Nick Pierce, Lauren Jarvis, Jane Roe, Anne Guillot. Design: Jo Chapman, Tim Lambert, Emily Hurlock. Publisher: Jonathan Grogan. Production: Jim Bulley. Photos/illustrations: Shutterstock.com, Rawpixel.com, Michelle Urra, Alex Bailey. Colour origination by GMC Reprographics. Printed and bound in China.